TALES FROM THE
NEW YORK RANGERS
LOCKER ROOM

A COLLECTION OF THE GREATEST
RANGERS STORIES EVER TOLD

BY
GILLES VILLEMURE
AND
MIKE SHALIN

FOREWORD BY ED GIACOMIN

SPORTS
PUBLISHING

Sports Publishing books may be purchased in bulk at special discounts for
sales promotion, corporate gifts, fund-raising, or educational purposes. Special
editions can also be created to specifications. For details, contact the Special Sales
Department, Sports Publishing, 307 West 36th Street, 11th Floor, New York,
NY 10018 or sportspubbooks@skyhorsepublishing.com.

Sports Publishing® is a registered trademark of Skyhorse Publishing, Inc.®,
a Delaware corporation.

Visit our website at www.sportspubbooks.com.

10 9 8 7 6 5 4 3

Library of Congress Cataloging-in-Publication Data

Names: Villemure, Gilles, 1940- | Shalin, Mike, 1954-
Title: Tales from the New York Rangers locker room : a collection of the greatest
Rangers stories ever told / [by Gilles Villemure and Mike Shalin; foreword by Ed
Giacomin]
Other titles: Gilles Villemure's tales from the Ranger locker room
Description: New York : [Champaign, Ill.], [2016]
Identifiers: LCCN 2016005997| ISBN 9781613219034 (alk. paper) | ISBN
   9781613219065 (Ebook)
Subjects: LCSH: New York Rangers (Hockey team)--History. | New York Rangers
   (Hockey team)--Anecdotes. | Villemure, Gilles, 1940-
Classification: LCC GV848.N43 V55 2016 | DDC 796.962/64097471--dc23 LC
record available at http://lccn.loc.gov/2016005997

Cover design by Tom Lau
Cover photo credit AP Images

ISBN: 978-1-61321-903-4
Ebook ISBN: 978-1-61321-906-5

Printed in the United States of America

For my mom and dad, who supported and followed me from the first day I played hockey, and to my wife and children—I love you all!

—G.V.

For Mary and my sons, Joshua, Taylor, and Mackenzie

—M.S.

For all the heroes of September 11— we will NEVER forget!

Contents

Foreword

by Ed Giacomin

Gilles Villemure is probably the most honest individual I've ever been associated with.

The man's word was his bond. I've valued that quite a bit because we've had very many different dealings, and he's always come through a hundred percent. I knew him a long time before we actually played in the National Hockey League together. He's just one fine individual.

Hockey was his love. Horse racing was his passion—but when he got to the game he was all business.

It took Gilles a long time to make it to the NHL, but like myself, coming from Canada and living hockey your whole life, you didn't want to be a failure. He wanted to be a very successful story, and by sticking it out, eventually it paid off for him just like it paid off for me.

The hardest thing for both myself and for Gilles when we got to the Rangers is that both of us wanted to play. But I was more open and more critical about it because I always said that I should be playing. That's me, and if I didn't say that I have no business being in sports. Gilles was the type of a person who *wanted* to play but could accept not playing, which I found was a little bit different. When he did play, he gave you 100 percent and he always performed very, very well. I admired him so much because I found it very hard thinking: how can he play like that and play so well while not playing as much?

He was a unique character, and that's why we became such a good team. He probably resented the fact that I played so much, but he was able to accept it, and the greatest thing is when we won the Vezina Trophy together.

I never asked him if he wanted to go somewhere where he could play every day. That never crossed our minds. I know it never crossed my mind. I just felt that he accepted that role and he was able to perform so well in it. He had a passion for horses, so that was kind of an out for him—so if he knew I was playing Wednesday night, he could go out Tuesday night and go to the track. That was unique. It was different, and if anything should have happened to me, he was always ready.

You have to be a special person to be able to take on that kind of a role and not be bitter about it—he always had an open mind, he was always flamboyant, and he was always very happy. Whatever the team did, he was always 100 percent for it.

—Ed Giacomin, June 2002

Preface

So much has happened to the Rangers and the game I love since we first wrote this book.

After all, it has been over a decade.

The biggest change regarding the Rangers is that there is now another "new" Garden. Well, it is actually the same building sitting proudly between Seventh and Eighth Avenues, but it is only the same on the outside.

For a hockey player who started his NHL career in the old place up on 50th Street and Eighth Avenue, which was primitive by today's standards, what they've done with "today's" Madison Square Garden is amazing.

When asked for one word about the renovated Garden, I just say, "Outstanding."

The seats are great. The view is wonderful from anywhere. There are beautiful suites all over the rink and we get to see them when we visit our sponsors. It's just gorgeous. It's night and day from what it used to be.

It seems the lighting on the ice is better and they have fixed the problems with the ice. It's cooler in the building, which has to help the ice; you need a sweater when you're sitting there.

The scoreboard is huge—very impressive. The suites are beautiful; it's hard to believe when you see it. The lobby is beautiful. You've got more room on the concourses. They did a hell of a job.

They put a lot of money into the place, and it was money well spent. It's hard to describe how beautiful it is to anyone who hasn't been there. If you're a Rangers fan and you haven't seen the place, add it to your bucket list.

Our Game

We suffered through a lockout that killed the 2004–05 season and took the spirit out of hockey fans everywhere, but the game is back and more popular than ever. Hockey is a wonderful game, and the players playing it today are so talented.

Hockey was always popular, but it's even more popular now. There are a lot of contributing factors, but one big thing is that the game is everywhere now. There are franchises thriving in places you never connected with hockey. And around the world? Players are coming from everywhere now, whereas in the past players used to come mostly from Canada because that's what we did; we went outside and skated all day. We had outdoor rinks and it was 30, 40 below and we just skated.

Now, it seems like every country has adopted hockey. Look at the excitement generated by the Olympics, where the teams from small countries have been scaring the traditional powers.

College hockey is also more popular and played by more colleges than ever.

The game today also gets faster all the time. The players are bigger, while the rinks are the same size; thus, the game is now so much tougher to play. There is no room and you have to do everything faster. You don't have the time—you get the puck and you have to get rid of it right away. They used to carry the puck more in my day, but now they have to dump it in and go after it quickly.

Another change is that in the past, a defenseman used to be able to grab on to a player coming at him and get away with it. Now, if you do anything it's a penalty. The skill guys have more room because they can't be grabbed, but they run out of room quickly; you just have to think and make the right move.

The game also takes less time. They took out the red line and that makes for fewer offsides stoppages. But it's hard to carry the puck now. The defensemen are 6–5, 6–6, 6–7, and it's very hard to carry the puck into the zone. The kids are bigger than we were. There's no room.

So many things are incredible for the players now, too, and I'm not even talking about the salaries. For example, the traveling is better; we used to take buses and go into airports to take commercial flights and now there are charters. Lastly, there are better TV deals, since more people are watching the game than ever before.

The Cap

The league is doing very well now because of the salary cap.

The Montreal Canadiens, when we were kids, used to get all the players. Now, the system is set up for parity, where every team has a chance. Teams can no longer stockpile players or hide them in the minors. Every team has a set amount it can spend. The Canadiens have the same cap as the San Jose Sharks and as the Arizona Coyotes.

It gives everyone the same playing field. Yes, some teams still spend more than others—it's amazing that Jonathan Toews and Patrick Kane are both making $10 million a year. Sidney Crosby is making $12 million. These players are worth it, but it makes it tougher on their teams because they still have to fit the rest of their roster in under the cap.

There is free agency, and the July 1 start of free agency keeps hockey in the news in the summer as well.

As an old guy who made a lot less than the players are making today, let me say this: it's GREAT! The sport is thriving and these guys deserve what they're getting.

The guys can now skate all year 'round because they don't have to go get other jobs. They have a shorter training camp, but they don't need it as much as we did, since they have been skating all summer and they come to camp early and are ready by the start of camp. They show up a month early and just skate.

They also have the facilities that we didn't have—the work-out machines, trainers, etc., all of which is geared toward getting the players in perfect shape for the start of the season. They have video and even kitchens in the training facilities. The sticks are also getting better every day, making life a little tougher for the goalie.

It's like anything else—the equipment keeps evolving. Like the bats in baseball, they're lighter and livelier.

All the equipment is better. There are more guys now who can shoot a puck harder than our guys did in the seventies.

We had some hard shooters, like the Hulls, who would shoot it on the fly. The thing that helped Bobby Hull was the curved stick. He would fire that puck with that stick and it would do all kinds of things. So many of these guys today can fire the puck like the best guys we had.

I never minded playing the hard shot. I was an angle goaltender and I didn't mind challenging the shooter. We worked together with our defensemen, telling them, *let us handle the shot and you take the other guy.* I think that's the same today as it was in our day.

The Overtime

When we first did this book, the NHL had been using a five-minute 4-on-4 overtime period to decide games. Then, they brought in the shootout—and goalies love the shootout because that's what we always did after practice, anyway.

I love the shootout. I've always loved it.

On game days, after practice, six, seven, eight guys would stay and we would have shootouts. We practiced that a lot. Now, the goaltenders are so good (not that we weren't good back in the day) that the averages are on their side in these things to stop the shots, really.

The goalies, like the players, are bigger, and they have great equipment now. Goaltending coaches have also made a big difference. Even the masks are much better (you'll see my mask elsewhere in these pages). You take a guy like Henrik Lundqvist, he's a great goalie and he even uses his head to stop the puck sometimes. The pads are also bigger and lighter; we used to wear these heavy leather pads and they would get soaked and get so heavy.

As I mentioned previously with regard to the defensemen, the kids are bigger than we were in our day. Even the goalies average about 6–2 now and cover so much more of the net.

3-on-3 Overtime

This year brought another rules change to the game, and this is one I love as well.

People were unhappy that too many 4 on 4s were ending without a team scoring and then they would have the shootout. They wanted to cut down on shootouts, so they went to a 3-on-3 matchup in overtime.

When it's 3 on 3, you better not miss your check or they're going to go the other way 3 on 2. If you come down the wing and fire a shot, you better hit the net or the puck is going to fly all the way around the boards and they're on their way down to the other end.

The Rangers just had a game early in the 2015–16 season where Derek Stepan hit the crossbar, the puck bounced out, and the Devils were on their way to a 2 on 1 and won the hockey game.

I saw it and liked it right away.

I don't know if the goaltenders like it, but it's entertaining for the fans and it does cut down on shootouts. They tried it in the minor leagues and it worked and I think it's going to be great for the NHL.

People ask me how I would feel about it if they had it when I was playing, and I say that I wouldn't have minded it at all.

It's even for both sides. Both sides have to be very careful that they don't let the other team take the puck and go the other way, but if they do, the goaltender has to stop the puck. That's what he gets paid for.

Even before the shootout, we used to practice 2 on 1s all the time. I used to tell the guys to bring them and I'll be ready.

We used to practice that a lot—Brad Park was an offensive defenseman and I used to tell Brad to go up the ice, don't worry about a 2 on 1 against us. I will handle it.

We had skill players who did their best work taking the puck up the ice. I told them not to worry about it. Eddie (Giacomin) was the same way. It's our job to be up to the challenge and to be ready to cover them.

These goalies today—Lundqvist, Carey Price, all those guys—make some unbelievable saves, and goalies thrive on that. We did in my day, and they still thrive on it today.

The Fans

One thing that hasn't changed is the passion of the Rangers fans. They were great to us in my day; they went wild when we did well and they let us have it when we didn't. But they were always there for us.

They still are, and now they have that beautiful redesigned Madison Square Garden to go to. The prices are high, but they keep coming; they're the greatest fans in sports!

And they never forget. I'm seventy-five years old now, and they still know who I am. They still talk to me on the train. This is a whole new generation of fans, but Rangers fans are deep in the history of the club and it's great to be part of that history.

We were very popular way back in the seventies and now, forty or fifty years later, they still know who we are.

Even out on Long Island, where I live, the people know me. When I started there were no Islanders and everyone on the Island were Rangers fans. Now, they still go to the game.

Mike Shalin asked me how I feel about the Islanders leaving Long Island for Brooklyn and I think it's a wait-and-see thing. I know Islanders fans think they were deserted by the team and it's tough when your team moves away. But at least they didn't move to another state. They're in Brooklyn, and the real fans will keep going to the game.

Who knows—maybe they'll get used to it. The Islanders are an up-and-coming young hockey team and I think their real fans will be at the game. They will also pick up new fans coming to that new building in Brooklyn.

Henrik Lundqvist

One word to describe Henrik Lundqvist? Unbelievable. It's just that simple.

I've seen a lot of great goaltenders in my lifetime, including Mike Richter, Giacomin, Gerry Cheevers, Bernie Parent, Ken Dryden, all those guys—but this guy is so steady. He's been doing that for years.

I'm prejudiced. I like all the goaltenders. Mike Richter? What can you say, one Stanley Cup in seventy-five years and he's the guy who did it. He's in the Hall of Fame. But Lundqvist? Believe me, I'm a fan.

He's very steady. The style is different; we stood up a lot more, whereas these guys cover the bottom of the net.

Is Lundqvist the best there is today? I see Lundqvist and Carey Price as the top two right now. Hey, you make the NHL because you are good, and right now I'll go with Lundqvist and Price. Price is unbelievable.

I watched a game between the Rangers and Canadiens and both goalies were great. I was jealous at how good they were. Sometimes I watch myself on old films and I criticize myself, why I didn't do some things differently. But the goaltender coaches have been great for today's goaltenders. They see all the replays and work with their goalies on the video. We didn't do that.

I didn't know what I was doing. I mean, I knew what I was doing but didn't have someone telling me what I was doing wrong. These guys, like the goaltenders in my day, are great, but they have that advantage of having a goalie coach and not being on their own.

Introduction

by Gilles Villemure

The date was June 14, 1994—a special spot on the calendar every Ranger fan should have etched into his or her brain. On that very special night, the New York Rangers ended the curse and tasted the thrill of winning the Stanley Cup for the first time since 1940, ending the questions and the horrible chants of "nine-teen, for-ty, nine-teen, for-ty."

I didn't play for the Rangers that night—when Mark Messier, Brian Leetch, Mike Richter, & Co. finally brought it home—I had retired from hockey in 1977, seventeen years earlier, and had left the Rangers two years prior to that. But I was there with those guys on that special night, and it's a night I'll never forget.

Remember the words from that song in *West Side Story*, about being a Jet? That's the way it is when you're a Ranger—you're a Ranger till your last dying day. Special team. Special place.

If you've forgotten—and if you're reading this book, the chances are there's no way you'll ever forget—the Rangers, who had survived the New Jersey Devils after Messier's incredible guarantee and personal follow-through in Game 6 and Stephane Matteau's wraparound goal in Game 7, won three of the first four games against the Vancouver Canucks in the finals. The Cup was finally going to be ours. But the Canucks won Games 5 and 6, and a Game 7 was necessary—at the Garden.

The Rangers set up a special alumni area for that game, down near the glass. I was there. So was Rod Gilbert. And Steve Vickers. And Walter Tkaczuk—four teammates who had come so close to winning the Cup with the Rangers, reaching the finals in 1972 and losing to the Bruins. We were all there, in special seats right near the home penalty box on the 31st Street side of the Garden.

Later, I would read that Gilbert, perhaps the greatest Ranger of them all, said, "I hurt my hands thumping on the glass . . . and I lost my voice in English and French."

Marv Albert, the longtime Rangers announcer, said that night, "The Rangers win the Stanley Cup: words that a lot of people never thought they would hear in their lifetime." One fan held up a now-famous sign that read: "Now I can die in peace."

That's the way it is being a Ranger—or a Rangers fan. That's why I still get recognized on Long Island and at the Garden almost forty years after I finished playing. I grew up close to Montreal, in the town of Trois Rivieres (Three Rivers), Quebec, and people up there are crazy for the Canadiens. But Canadian loyalty to a hockey team is one thing—that's where the game was born. In New York, you're fighting with the other sports, but Ranger fans are a special breed. And on that night in 1994, they finally got their wish.

The Rangers haven't won the Cup since, and they've had some good teams. They reached the finals a couple of years ago, but they have always come up short—even with the Great

One, Wayne Gretzky, who ended his brilliant career wearing his No. 99 on Garden ice. He was reunited on Broadway with his Edmonton champion pal Mark Messier and there were some magic moments their second time together. The Rangers didn't win it all, but the fans were always there rooting for their team.

It's all part of being a Ranger, which I was for so much of my life.

About that life. I started skating at age five—and was able to live the dream of almost every Canadian boy—to grow up to be a real professional hockey player. I played 17 years of pro hockey, seven full years and parts of three others in the National Hockey League. I played five full seasons with the New York Rangers, two with the Chicago Blackhawks.

I am seventy-five years old now. I retired at age thirty-seven.

It took a lot of hard work, dedication, and commitment, along with a lot of hard knocks, to make it to the top, even sharing a Vezina Trophy with Eddie Giacomin in my first full year in the NHL. But along with the game I loved so much, I got to meet and know many great people and start friendships I hope I'll never forget or lose.

In the coming pages, I hope to share with you some of the things that happened to me in my hockey career, with a heavy emphasis on those five special years inside the Ranger locker room. I played with and against many great players and characters, and I will share some of that with you in these pages.

My coauthor, Mike Shalin, was a season ticket holder back when I came up, and like most Rangers fans, he can remember more than the players on some of these things. His insights will be intertwined and he will make all this make some sense, because . . . well, I stopped hockey pucks for a living and did a lot of it without wearing a mask. But I got more help on this book—you will read chapters throughout the book under the title, "With a Little Help From My Friends," and then read the words of some of my teammates and of our leader, the great Emile Francis. I think that all of this will take you back to a special time.

The Beginning

I belonged to the Rangers when I was sixteen, when I signed a "C" Form that tied me to them. Years ago, there were no draft choices. It was just sign a "C" Form and you belonged to that team. I was playing hockey in my hometown and the Rangers had a scout, Yvan Prud'homme, come to see me for a few games. He liked what he saw and asked me to sign the form. That was it—my long career with the New York Rangers organization was under way. I was sixteen then and stayed with the Rangers until I was thirty-five, when I was traded to the Chicago Blackhawks for the last two years of my career.

What a thrill! They gave me $100 to sign that form and a $500 bonus when I made the pros, which I did with the Vancouver Canucks (they were a minor-league team then) in 1962. Imagine that—a hundred bucks to sign and five hundred when I turned pro—we're talking hundreds here, not thousands or millions. You think the game has changed at all today?

I got that money and thought they were really giving me something. But the money aside, they gave me the chance to do what I loved—play hockey. I arrived as a pro when there were only six teams in the NHL, and I needed expansion and the faith of Emile Francis to finally make it to the league on a full-time basis in 1970. It was a long haul, but I wouldn't trade it for anything, because being a hockey player is what I always wanted, and to be able to play in the National Hockey League? Wow! And I was able to step into a lineup that was on the verge of greatness, a team that would come so close to winning the Stanley Cup that would elude the franchise for two more decades before that great night in 1994.

Introduction

by Mike Shalin

Through much of his time with the New York Rangers, Gilles Villemure may have heard a voice from above calling down to him at Madison Square Garden. That voice, which came from Section 440, Row A, Seat 10 in the mezzanine, now has the great pleasure of working with the former Rangers goaltender on this book.

As a former Rangers season ticket holder in Section 440, I saw Villemure join Ed Giacomin and form the best one-two goaltending punch in the National Hockey League. I saw Villemure not only lighten the load on Giacomin but also get more than one person saying the newcomer was the actual No. 1. Now, all these years later, it's with great pleasure that I get to help Villemure share his and, yes, even some of my own *Tales from the New York Rangers Locker Room.*

A book like this is a labor of love for someone like me, someone who once attended 110 straight games at Madison Square Garden. The day my brother got married, March 1, 1970, I had to slip out to the parking lot to find out what the Rangers and Blackhawks were doing (Chicago won). I just couldn't completely stay away. A crazy fan who once had a rubber chicken in a noose with Derek Sanderson's number on the back, attended road games, waited for autographs, did all those kinds of things. I used to run a goal-scoring pool in my section, and I kept a detailed scrapbook on the yearly doings of this team (some of it is illustrated in these pages). Later, after Villemure left for Chicago and then for retirement, I wound up covering the team for both United Press International and the *New York Post* before moving to Boston in 1983. Most of my years since have been spent away from covering the sport I love so much, but the close ties never go away. Now, getting to do this book with one of *my* Rangers brings me back home—to New York and the team I love.

As a fan, I met the Ranger PR team of John and Janet Halligan, always friendly and helpful to us as we passed through the press box after games as fans, giving us extra sets of what we considered to be precious press notes and stats that detailed everything we needed to know. Both were helpful when I jumped the line from fan to writer, making press credentials available for young journalists whenever possible. John, who always had kind words for others, has passed away, and the hockey world misses him.

There are others to thank on a long road that leads to a book like this. The late Norman MacLean, one of the true characters of the hockey world, was always there at the beginning, always helping me get my foot in the door. There was Jill Knee out on Long Island, opening the Islanders press box to young guys like myself and future Rangers and Islanders broadcaster Howie Rose, another rabid nut in those days. And Stan Fischler, "The Maven," who helped get me started. There was Marv Albert, who was always helpful to young folks trying to make it in the business. Later, I worked with people like Sam Rosen, now one of the great voices of hockey, and Frank

Brown, the former outstanding hockey writer with the Associated Press and the New York *Daily News* who is now working as the NHL's head PR guy. On and on the list runs.

This hockey fan, who had the great pleasure of covering the miracle of Lake Placid hockey gold in 1980, became primarily a baseball and college sports writer as his career went on, but the love of hockey never left, which is what made it so easy to be a dad to three hockey-playing sons.

Finally, I'd like to thank the Rangers of my youth and teen years—one of them whose words you'll read in these pages. The Rangers didn't win the Stanley Cup back then, but they provided plenty of entertainment for so many of us. And here's hoping these pages provide even more. Enjoy!

 ## Testing Your Ranger Knowledge

Throughout these pages, at the ends of the first 10 chapters, you will find questions—10 of them—that will truly test your knowledge of the New York Rangers. If you can get six or seven of these without looking, you know your Rangers stuff. If you get more than that, you're a Rangers genius.

"I was in hockey fifty years, from the day I started to the day I quit—and that group of people that I had from about '70 through '76, they were the best bunch of players that I've ever seen in my life, that I ever played with or ever handled.

"The thing about them is there was nobody jealous of one another. They were a team through and through. There was no one player concerned about what the other guy was making. Nobody was jealous because one guy was getting more ice time than the other guy. They knew what their jobs were—if I was killing penalties, if I was on the power play . . . they were really a group that got along well together, and that's what made them as good as they were. In order to win the Stanley Cup, you gotta be good and you gotta be lucky, and we sure as hell weren't lucky."

—Emile Francis on his teams during the first half of the seventies, perhaps the best team ever that never won a Stanley Cup

1

Getting Started

A Little About Me

I started playing in goal when I was fourteen. One goaltender got hurt—we had outside rinks in Three Rivers, 20 below, 30 below every day—and I used to be a forward, a good forward. I used to win the scoring championship. But the goaltender got hurt, I went in, and that was it. I stayed in goal for the next twenty-three years.

But I remember that I froze. You're not moving around and I didn't get that many shots, so I stood still a lot. When it's 20 degrees below zero and you're not moving . . . I'll never forget, I was cold! But I played. I lived through it.

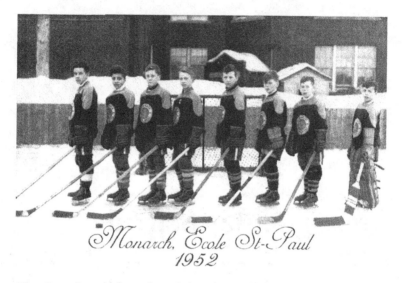

Monarch, École St-Paul
1952

Here I am (second from the right) at age twelve before I started playing goal. (Gilles Villemure)

I was good and they came after me. But my dad had to find out if I was good enough. They sent me to Troy, Ohio, when I was seventeen. I couldn't speak English. They sent me there for three or four weeks, I played three or four games in the Eastern Pro League—I guess they called it that—and I went back home and did my Junior "B" when I was eighteen and my Junior "A" when I was nineteen, with Guelph, Ontario. Then I went on.

Years ago, we had no education. The kids now can go to college and then go on to the National Hockey League. We didn't even think about college when I played as a kid—nobody went to college—nobody. There was no college then. People are always asking why it took so long—after 1952—for Canada to win another gold medal. Well, for so many of those years, college kids represented the country, and in most cases the reason they were in college was that they weren't good enough to go on and play in the NHL. There's one major change between those days and now.

Who Else Could I Root For?

Growing up in Quebec and being a French-Canadian, there was really only one hockey team I could root for—the beloved Montreal Canadiens.

No real choice here—the Habs—Maurice Richard, Jean Beliveau, Boom Boom Geoffrion, Bert Olmstead, Jacques Plante . . . we didn't have television then; I was a young kid, and I would just listen to the radio every night. I was a Montreal Canadiens fan 100 percent.

My first memory of that team and those players was how good they were. They were something else. What a team they had. They used to say, "Boomer's taking a slap shot from the point and it goes right through the goaltender." I'll never forget them. I was ten or eleven years old, and I was seventy miles from Montreal, but I never got there as a kid. In Trois Rivieres (Three Rivers), I used to go watch the juniors or the seniors play—that was pro then. I used to watch the games at home.

But we couldn't afford to go to Montreal when I was a kid. I'm the oldest of three brothers, and it was tough—my father worked his butt off, but he wasn't making much money. That's why when the Rangers came in with the "C" Form and gave me a hundred dollars, I jumped. I said, "Give it to me now." A hundred dollars is *big* money. That was huge—I had never seen a hundred dollars in my life and I was fifteen or sixteen years old.

I quit school when I was seventeen years old, but my dad had to ask everyone around if I had a chance to make it. "Is he good enough to make it?" I guess the answer to that turned out to be "yes."

Junior Hockey

I played junior hockey in Guelph, Ontario, for a farm team of the New York Rangers. I was there for one year, 1958.

Two of my teammates there were Rod Gilbert and Jean Ratelle. Since I could not speak a word of English, Rod and Jean, who were also French-Canadian, were able to help me through that year. They had been there two years before I got there.

From junior league, they went to the National Hockey League, and I went to the Long Island Rovers in the Eastern League. We were reunited a few times over the next several years, and for good as teammates for the Rangers in 1970. We played five more years together.

Traveling Man

In the 1960–61 season, I played in the Eastern Hockey League for the New York Rovers. What an experience that was.

We used to travel by bus from Commack, Long Island, to Nashville, Knoxville, Charlotte, Johnstown (Pennsylvania), etc. We would play seven games in eight nights, travel hundreds of miles between games, and travel all day to play a game at seven o'clock that night. Many times, we got to the game late, and when we got there our equipment was always damp because we only had one set and had no time to dry it because of the bus trips.

The Long Island Arena in Commack was our home rink. It was sold out for every game. The fans were great. Remember, there were only six teams in the National Hockey League at the time, so if you wanted to be a hockey fan, you had to take it anywhere you could get it—and these people came to the arena every night for our games.

Instead of glass behind the goal, the Long Island Arena had chicken wire, and the side boards had nothing to protect the fans. People would be sitting behind the boards and they used to grab the opposition's players to slow them down. The players would get so mad they would jump into the stands and fight with the fans. It was crazy.

The rink was dark, the ice was not as bright as it is today, and the ice wasn't painted. The players would make snow with their skates in front of my net, which would enable me to see the puck a little better. It wasn't that long of a ride into Manhattan, but this place was light-years away from Madison Square Garden (it was the old Garden back then, the one on 8th Avenue and 50th Street).

I was the only goaltender on our team and had no backup. In 1960, I wasn't wearing a mask. One night, I broke my nose during a game. They took me to the dressing room, where the doctor sat me down, put my head against a wall, and with his two big hands pushed my nose back into place. Then, without batting an eyelash, he said to me, "You're ready to go back on the ice." I went back on the ice and finished the game. Those were the days.

The Old Garden

I played my first games for the Rangers in 1963—at the old Garden on 8th Avenue and 49th–50th Streets. It was an old rink that was on its way out, and we actually had to practice upstairs.

First, we had to get dressed on the main floor in our regular locker room, and then we had to walk to the second floor to the practice rink. We would have our skate guards on for the walk to the second floor.

To go on the ice, we had to jump the boards. But on one particular day, I forgot to take my skate guards off—something every kid in youth hockey has done once or twice in his or her life—and I took a dive and almost broke my back. The guys got a kick out of that one.

The boards in this rink were aluminum, and every time a shot hit them it sounded like an explosion. Practice was an hour and a half long and you'd leave the ice with a headache every day. Think the players were happy when they built the new place a few years later?

Fred Shero

Obviously, Emile Francis was the coach who had the greatest impact on my hockey career and my life. But the second guy, right behind him, would be Freddie Shero.

Shero coached me in the American Hockey League in Buffalo when we won a championship—the Calder Cup. He was great—and he went to Philadelphia after that and won two Stanley Cups.

Here I am during the 1967–68 season, when I played for Fred Shero at Buffalo in the American Hockey League. (Gilles Villemure)

Here's the mask I started wearing in 1966 (left) next to the kind they wear today. Pretty different, huh? (Gilles Villemure)

He had hockey sense. I don't know if the guy knew how to write, but he had hockey sense. He knew everything. Even little, minor things. He would put an extra guy out on the ice at the end of a game, put six guys out, seven guys out. Seven? I know that sounds crazy, but he did it. We scored. Seven guys—oh, yeah—eight guys sometimes. He got away with it. I don't know how, but he did.

He'd take somebody else's stick on the other team and throw it on the ice, the other team would get a penalty for having an extra stick on the ice. That's right, just grab one of their sticks from next to the bench and throw it on the ice. They'd get a penalty.

He had more tricks than you could ever imagine. The stuff he used to do was unbelievable.

People ask me if Freddie was strange. Strange? No, he wasn't. Not strange. He was funny. In the American Hockey League, we used to go by bus all the time—we never took a plane, never. We'd have a four-hour trip, a three-and-a-half-hour trip, and he'd be sitting in the front. After half an hour, everybody would be up in the front listening to him. I'm talking about stories here, not jokes, but stories. Everybody would listen to him. He was unreal.

We had a great team in Buffalo. We didn't have a lot of guys who played in the NHL, but in 1969–70, we won everything. I think we lost about 10 games, and I had eight shutouts and a 2.52 goals-against average to lead the league. I also had a 2.13 in the playoffs, which was the best in the AHL. We just had a great year.

And Freddie was right there at the front, teaching us things, tricking the opposition and the referees—and helping us win. It was no surprise to anyone that he went on to become such a great coach in the National Hockey League.

Putting On the Mask

I didn't wear a mask until I was twenty-six years old. In the mask you sweat a lot, and the sweat gets in your eyes and everything, and you can't breathe. It's a pain. But it has its obvious benefits, which is why I finally went to one in 1966.

Jacques Plante was the first goalie to put one on in an NHL game, and they didn't want him to wear it. But as the shots kept getting harder, one by one the goalies fell. I think Andy Brown was the last holdout, but Gump Worsley was one of the last guys to brave it without a mask.

Before the mask, I got hurt pretty bad a couple of times. I was in training camp without the mask on and I fell down. Jimmy Neilson got the puck and he fell on my head, and all my teeth went down my throat. I asked, "Where's my teeth?" I went to the bench and Frank Paice, the longtime Ranger trainer, was there. I said, "Frank, where's my teeth?" He pushed them all back in and I went back and played. They aren't my real teeth, but they were in the back of my throat—and Frank on the bench just snapped them back on and I went back in the net.

The other time, I broke my nose when I was with the Long Island Ducks. I heard a snap and I said, "Geez." My nose was over to the side. I had gotten hit with a stick and didn't have a mask. I remember a big doctor in the locker room said, "Come here, Gilly, put your head against the wall." I'll never forget that. He said, "Don't move." He pushed my nose right back in and said, "Okay, you're ready."

I was with the Rangers in camp in 1966. I wound up playing 70 games in Baltimore that year. I didn't make the Rangers, but I decided to go to the mask because everyone else was starting to wear them. I had to put one on. And mine was different than just about any other. I opened up the eyes on my mask and opened up my mouth, because I couldn't breathe. When you're not used to a mask, you can't breathe and can't see, so I opened up my eyes and my mouth, like a smile.

But masks were different then. We only had masks over our faces—we had nothing over the top of our heads. I remember that during one game in Montreal, I put my head down, and the puck hit me on top of my head and I got twenty stitches. That's part of the game, though.

Stitches? Before the mask? Forget about it. I got hit many times. After I started wearing the mask, I got hit many, many times in the face and the mask protected me. The shots were getting harder, there were a lot of screen shots—you needed the protection. If you remember, Bruins goalie Gerry Cheevers used to draw stitches on his mask to show how many different cuts he would have had without his mask protecting his face.

Sure, I got hit before I went to the mask, but there was nothing major. There was nothing to my eyes—nothing serious—and I'm grateful for that. Guys got hurt—some seriously. But we didn't know any better. We just played goal, and if you got hurt, you got hurt. I never thought even once that I would have to quit because I got hit. Never. That's the way we grew up—we grew up without the mask and people thought we were crazy. But we just wanted to play hockey.

Plante put his mask on during a game after he'd gotten hit, and I think his coach, the great Toe Blake, told him to take it off. But he started something—and now, with the equipment they have, kids are lucky. Can you imagine standing in front of an Al MacInnis slapshot with nothing covering your face? Think about that. We had Bobby Hull to worry about. Everyone seems to shoot the puck hard now. The shots are harder, those shots are *coming,* and even with the mask, Mike Richter once suffered a fractured skull. Those kids can shoot these days. The game got bigger and the ice remained the same size. These guys are huge!

 **Rangers Trivia #1**

Who holds the Rangers record for power-play goals in a season?

2

A Little Help from My Friends
Emile Francis

"Everywhere Gilles Villemure went, he played well. The only thing was—it wasn't until the late fifties that you started using two goalkeepers. To me, I didn't want him there unless he was going to play. Having been a goalkeeper myself, I wanted to play. It would only stymie his development if you brought him up and he played 10 games here. That's why I'd bring in Simmons, Sawchuk—because I knew Giacomin was going to play 60 games. But then the time came when you were going to bring in Villemure and you wanted him to play and if not alternate, have him play his share. Guys come in today, eighteen, nineteen years old, and they figure they should step

Emile Francis always thought I was "a real good goalkeeper."
(New York Rangers)

right in the league. But when he came in, he was prepared to play.

"It was a funny thing. I don't think we were trying to hold him back. But I don't think people really realized how good he was because a couple of times, in deals that could have been, as far as I was concerned, key deals, I'd say, 'You need goalkeeping, and if we can make this guy move, I've got a goalkeeper who can play in the National League.' They'd say, 'Who?' I'd say, 'Villemure.' And you could never sell somebody in the idea that he was a National League goalkeeper. It was the darndest thing I'd ever seen—and to me, he was. I thought he was a real good goalkeeper.

"He is one of the best guys you could ever want to have on your hockey club. Wherever he played, he was the best goalkeeper in the league—and they loved having him when he played there. He just had to wait for his time to come in the National League, and he took advantage of it when it did."

On Bobby Orr's effect on the 1972 finals:

"If you remember, Boston got us down against Giacomin, and I put [Villemure] in there. He went in and he beat Boston right in Boston, and they came back, and the only reason they beat us is it was a nothing-nothing game and Boston had a power play. Bruce MacGregor, who was one of our best penalty killers, couldn't get it by Orr. Orr gave him that deke to the inside, stepped around the outside, and fired it into the net. There's only one guy who could make a move like that, and it was Orr."

On Villemure's style:

"Villemure was a stand-up goalkeeper. He played his angles. He never beat himself. If you're gonna beat Gilles

Villemure, you had to beat him; he didn't beat himself. He was an old-time goalkeeper. He was a goalkeeper along the lines of a Johnny Bower—he played the angles, he stood up, and if you're gonna beat him, beat him, go ahead."

On the Giacomin-Villemure team:

"One guy caught with his left hand, Giacomin, and the other guy caught with his right hand. Honest to God, sometimes I don't think shooters paid attention to it because it was unorthodox to see a goalkeeper who caught with his right hand. I think that fooled a lot of players. Villemure and Giacomin to us were like the old Boston Braves, when they Spahn and Sain and then the rain. One was a lefty, one was a righty, and that's what we had."

On that duo winning the Vezina Trophy:

"Obviously, it would have been great to win the Stanley Cup. But I was so proud when he and Giacomin won the Vezina Trophy. No matter what happened, they can't take that away from him. Gilles didn't have an easy time getting there, and to do something like this in his first full year in the league is a credit to both our goalkeepers and the team in front of them."

On coming so close to winning the Stanley Cup:

"We had a knack on that team of getting the wrong guy hurt at the wrong time. The year before Rolfe hit Ratelle, we were playing the Vancouver Canucks and beating them easily. The game meant nothing. This was in March—it always happened in March. The Saturday night before, they had a track meet at Madison Square Garden. They had to put on the stuff that they ran on, but it seeped through to the ice. Now, when we started that night there was a hole right to the left of Eddie Giacomin, right in the faceoff circle. They sprayed it three or four times. So here we are, late in the third period, the puck's shot in our end, Brad Park's going back to pick it up and steps right in the hole that they'd been filling all night. He lost his balance, went into the boards, and tore up his knee. All these goofy things happened."

On being second-class citizens at the Garden:

"Ned Irish, who started the New York Knicks, would never agree to put the floor down on the ice, so the Knicks would play Saturday night, and then they'd try to make that ice up fast. We always seemed to be on every other Sunday afternoon at one o'clock. The basketball game would be over at eleven at night and they had until one o'clock to have it ready for us to play. We were always away on Saturday and getting home at three in the morning. We'd get to the Garden at 10:30 a.m. and, Christ, I saw guys skate by with sparks flying (from the concrete) because there wouldn't be more than like an eighth of an inch of ice on there because they didn't have time to make it again.

"He wouldn't leave the ice in because he said it would be too cool on the basketball fans' asses, that's what it amounted to. We were being treated like second-class citizens, really. I was so teed off after the night Dale Rolfe got hurt, I was talking to the press, and I told them, 'You know, I've seen better ice on the roads of Saskatchewan, where I come from, than here at Madison Square Garden.' Irving Felt, who was chairman of the board, saw it in all the papers and he said, 'You know, as chairman of the board of Madison Square Garden, I'm insulted about what you said about the ice at Madison Square Garden.' I said, 'Well, I've been here at Madison Square Garden long before you. The ice was horseshit when I came, it's horseshit now, and it will be as long as we continue to do what we're doing.' I said, 'You go back to Saskatchewan, like I said, and you'll find out that the ice is better on the highways than what we have.'"

On trading younger players for veterans because they were close to winning:

"The thing then was that you had your protected list. We had a very good farm system, and I knew that if we didn't protect some of these guys we were going to lose them, that we had a chance to lose them for nothing. You would deal a guy that would bring you a guy that would maybe put you over the top in that particular year. That protected list is why you had to make some of those deals, because you end up with nothing, except $30,000, which is nothing. I dealt Syl Apps for Glen Sather, and what we were lacking at that time was a little aggressiveness, another guy to put on the checking line, and the guy was a good penalty killer. If we had kept Apps, Apps wasn't going to make the team, and when we go in to put our protected list that summer, we would have lost them."

On the highlight of all his years with the Rangers:

"First of all, I think it was the teams I had there in the seventies. That five-year span. When I took over the team they'd missed the playoffs nine out of ten years, and I remember the worst thing that happened to the Rangers before I got there was nobody wanted to play there. They dealt Bill Gadsby and Billy McNeill to Detroit for Red Kelly. Gadsby and McNeill took right off. They couldn't wait to go to Detroit. In the meantime, Red Kelly wouldn't come to New York, so a short time later, there's no deal. So the Rangers said, 'Hey, we want our guys back,' and they sent them back. Gadsby and McNeil had to go there, Kelly sat on his ass, and Toronto made a deal for Kelly. Toronto went on to win four Stanley Cups in five years. So, when I took over the Rangers, I started dealing left and right. I had two or three guys who said, 'Oh, no, we won't come to New York.' I said, 'Fine, sit on your ass, and after you miss a few paychecks, maybe you'll decide to come then.' They all came. The minute you build a competitive club, everybody wants to come, but you had to build a competitive team.

"I remember when I came to New York, [hearing] comments from players who said, 'We don't like playing in New York because nobody recognizes us.' I remember saying, 'I'll tell you what—if I missed the playoffs nine out of ten years, I wouldn't want anybody to recognize me.' But I said, 'They'll recognize us, they'll recognize us when we win!' And it's amazing when you build a competitive team how the people respond. Those, to me, were the best years of my life because it was worthwhile work. I never took a vacation, I worked and worked because it was for the sake of the team, but more for the sake of the fans because of the way they responded and supported you. So, the highlight to me is building a team and watching the way fans support the team."

On hearing that Ace Bailey wasn't even supposed to be on the ice when he scored the winning goal in Game 1 of the 1972 finals:

"I didn't know that. We were on the way to one of the greatest comebacks in playoff history. We were down 5–1, and we tied that thing up with about five minutes to go. We were controlling the play. We had beaten Chicago four in a row, and [the Bruins] were playing St. Louis, and we had to wait around a week for that series. You try everything, you give them a couple of days easy and then you work like hell, but that time of year, if you get that time off, you know you're going to have a tough time. We had to go open in Boston, and, Christ, they had us down 5–1. We came back and tied it, and then Bailey broke our backs with that goal. That, to me, if I looked at that whole series—and Bobby Orr's goal in the sixth game was a great goal—that goal there was a back-breaker. First game of the series, having come back from four goals back, and then to lose it like that . . . that was a tough loss."

On the Rangers finally winning the Stanley Cup:

"When the Rangers finally won against Vancouver, they went down to that seventh game. The faceoff was in the Ranger end, to the right of the net, and I think there were about 18 seconds left. I was doing the color for them on TV. I was standing down there in the runway, and I was looking up in the stands just to see the expressions on people's faces. Some of them were crying. The one guy had a sign that said everything: 'Now I Can Die In Peace.' That says it all right there."

On demanding the Rangers never lose a home playoff date to the circus:

"In 1950, the Rangers were in the finals against Detroit, and in those days, they got thrown out of the Garden because of the circus. They upset the Canadiens playing the last two games in Montreal, and the next series, against Detroit—five games in Detroit and two in Toronto. That's the Rangers' two home games. The last four were in Detroit, and the Rangers lost Game 7 in double overtime. Then, when I was getting the opportunity to take over the Rangers, I said under one condition. I remember Bill Jennings asked, 'What's that?' I said, 'Well, first of all, there's no more loyal fans than Ranger fans, and I'll never forget what happened in 1950—that's not fair to the fans, and it's sure as hell not fair to the players. I will have nothing to do with the New York Rangers unless you guarantee me we get in the playoffs, which we will, that we're going to get every home game that we're entitled to.' So, he says, 'I'll have to look into that before I can guarantee that,' and he talked to the circus. The circus is a big thing in April and May, and he said, 'The only problem is that they still want their three performances. If we're to do that, you'd have to play at 8:30.' And I said, 'I don't give a damn if we play at midnight, we want to play at home, in our building, and with our fans there.' And from that day on they've never lost a home game that they're entitled to."

On sharing the Garden with the circus—and the smell:

"Wasn't that beautiful? And I can remember my office was right under the fifth floor, and those animals are there for two months. One day I came into my office and guess what was coming right through the ceiling? Elephant piss. Right through the floor and the ceiling. My office smelled like a barn. After two months, it seeped right through the elevators, into the offices, the whole building."

On Villemure's other career:

"I go to Roosevelt Raceway one night, and who the hell do you think is racing? Villemure. People were telling me to bet on him. I said, 'No way, he's a goalkeeper, he's not a driver.' Guess what—he won the race."

 **Rangers Trivia #2**

Here's a goalie question:
As this book went off to press in February 2016,
Henrik Lundqvist was set to
break Mike Richter's Rangers record
for games played. Who is No. 3?

3

Glory Days

My Greatest Moment

It would be easy to look at my career and point to the Vezina Trophy or getting to the Stanley Cup finals as the highlights of my career. But I don't know about that. There are two or three things that I did that I'm proud of.

Individually, I won the Most Valuable Player in the American Hockey League two straight years, 1969 and 1970, before I came up and stayed with the Rangers. That was big. Then, we won the Calder Cup in the American Hockey League as a team and that was special. And then the Vezina Trophy—those three are pretty close together. Maybe the Most Valuable Player in the league two years in a row might be the top.

Remember, that was a time when I thought that might be as high as I would go. I was thirty years old. I thought I was finished. Do you know how many guys there are who stay in the American Hockey League that never make it to the NHL but were good enough to make it to the NHL? There were only so many teams.

I was happy when they expanded. But I was thirty years old by 1970. I never thought I was going to make the NHL. I knew I had great years the last two years I played in the American Hockey League. MVP in the league two years in a row— you cant go any higher than that. But I was making $15,000 a year in 1969 and didn't know it would ever get better than that. I was living on that—I had no choice.

But Emile Francis gave me a chance. I took that chance, and I played seven years after that in the NHL because of Emile. If it wasn't for Emile Francis, I might never have made it. Who else is going to pick me up at thirty years old? Nowadays, thirty years old is old. But I made it from thirty to thirty-seven years old, and he's the one who gave me the break. Maybe I deserved it because of the two years I had, but still, I needed somebody to give me the break, and Emile did it.

He followed me closely the last year I was in the minors. He was in Buffalo all the time. Imagine that.

Cat's Team

Because it was so hard for Emile Francis to be both coach and general manager, he tried to give up coaching—three times.

Here I am talking with two of the greats. That's me on the left, with Maurice "The Rocket" Richard (center) and Emile Francis. (Gilles Villemure)

First, it was Bernie "Boom Boom" Geoffrion. Then, Larry Popein. Finally, Ron Stewart, the only one of the three who didn't wind up giving the job back to The Cat, who got fired when John Ferguson took over.

When the change was made from Popein during the 1973–74 season, it was clear to everyone we just played better under Emile. We turned things around.

"This can be a turning point for us," Bruce MacGregor said back then. "This is Emile's team; he's good for us. It's a much easier situation for all of us now that he's back." This was always Emile's team.

Emile Francis

When people ask me about Emile Francis, the main thing I say is he was a man who was just *living* hockey.

I'll never forget the way the man used to work. He was our coach and general manager, and we used to take charter flights out of town, and he was in front of the plane, always working. He was always writing something down—I don't know what he was writing, but he was always writing.

I remember once that after flying into a city when we got to our hotel, our rooms weren't ready. Emile got so mad. He said, "Let's get out of here. We're going somewhere else." That was it, we went somewhere else. Everything has to be ready. Everything has to be on time—if you're not on time, you miss the bus, take a cab. You had to be there.

Everything had to be just right—that's just the way he ran things—and he ran the whole show.

He lived hockey, he knew his hockey, knew who we were playing against. He had a system that was unbelievable—and the best thing is that everybody was following that system. And we had the greatest years the Rangers ever had.

Emile was great—he would cover up everything for everybody. If a guy got in trouble on the road—there were a lot of single guys on our team and sometimes things happen—he would say "I'll take care of it," and he did.

He used to call the referees all kinds of things. "You hot dogs," that was his favorite thing. "You hot dog, you."

Emile Francis deserved the Stanley Cup, and I know every player on those teams would say the same thing. He's the best I've seen. And now, when we get together with him, we're always talking to him about all the things we did on and off the ice, and he can't believe the stories. When he was a coach, he wasn't looking for anything; "Do your job on the ice, then there's no problem, and if you get in trouble off the ice, I'll take care of it." How many guys will do that for you? It's incredible, what he did for a couple of guys that got in trouble, got in big trouble, and he took care of it. That's the kind of guy he was.

He hated losing. I remember the year we lost against the Islanders, our last year together as a group, he was very upset. We came back from a 3–0 deficit, and we tied them up. He was upset, not about the players, but that fluky goal—the puck went over somebody's stick to J. P. Parise, blind, and it went in.

I started that game. The night before, I played against the Islanders, and we beat them out on the Island, 8–3, and I hurt my knee. It wasn't too bad. I started the game. We were down 3–0, The Cat took me out, which was the right thing to do, we tied up the game and a fluky goal beat us. He was upset. He was down.

I'll never forget—I saw his face coming into the locker room, and the man was out. He worked so hard all year, and all of a sudden a fluky goal beats you and that's it. And, as it turned out, those would be our last playoffs together because they started breaking the team up the next year.

The guy deserved a Stanley Cup. He did everything possible; he had a lot of good years.

Now, when we talk to him about the team, he doesn't shut up. He just loves to talk about it with us. I remember I was at a golf outing; Brad Park was standing with us, Steve Vickers, Rod Gilbert, and Vic Hadfield. We were talking about those years, the good times, off-the-ice stuff, he was listening and taking it all in. The thing is how hard we worked for him. And you know what? He was shaken—he knew the guys worked hard for him, but the way we were talking, he appreciated that.

His players were his players. They respected him; they worked very hard for him. That's just the way it was. What a man!

Money Talks

In 1972, we were in Oakland on a long road trip and Emile Francis called me into his hotel room. It was around 11:30 a.m. Boy, did I get scared. I thought he was going to give me bad news, like being traded.

Much to my surprise and elation, Emile had a new contract offer for me and he was waiting in his room for me to sign it. This was back in the days when not too many guys had agents to help them with their contract and you dealt with your club directly.

I was making $45,000 a year when I walked into that Oakland hotel room, and it took me a long time in hockey to get to that level. The new contract offer was for $90,000 a year for three years. That was a $270,000 deal. This was the time the WHA was threatening the NHL, and hockey players started getting a bit more—but double? Wow! What a surprise! I didn't even know what to say to Emile. I told him I'd be back in an hour with my answer. I think I must have been in shock.

Half an hour later, I went back to see him, and I don't know why, but I said, "I want ninety-five." I wanted him to make it $95,000 a year for three years. I don't know why I asked for the extra $5,000, because I knew I was happy with $90,000 (I was doubling my salary, for God's sake), but Emile just said, "No problem—sign the damn thing and I'll change it." I guess I did it because $95,000 was MY choice.

Thank you, Emile.

I really was stunned to get that kind of money. My paycheck more than doubled in one morning—and it was retroactive back to the start of the season. This was in November, I think.

That was *big* money.

But the money was there, and the salaries had been so low. You had agents coming into the game at the time and that drove Emile crazy. He hated agents and thought they were killing the league. We didn't have agents before that and the salaries were low, but that was all changing for the better.

I didn't have an agent, but to get that kind of money I guess I didn't need an agent. I was thrilled.

I have heard that all the big contracts our players were signing back then made us a fat-cat team. But we still played well for a year or so. Then, I don't know what happened after that—just before they traded everybody, we went flat! The team went flat. For what reason, I don't know. I never found out why, but it happened, and we just weren't the same.

Eddie Giacomin

Eddie Giacomin and I shared the goaltending duties for the Rangers for five years, and we were dealt out of New York the same week in 1975.

At first, I felt Eddie was a little uncomfortable. He was used to playing all the time and here I was ready to share his time. But as time went on, he got used to sharing it with me. Eddie played 55 percent of the game and I played 45 percent. When time came for the playoffs, Eddie was ready.

"It's no fun sitting on the bench; you want to be out there all the time," Eddie said after we settled into the new system and did so well. "But if it helps the team, then I'm all for it. That's what means the most to me."

And it did help the team—we won the Vezina Trophy our first year together, the Rangers' first Vezina since Davey Kerr won it in 1940.

"I knew in training camp that Eddie and Gilles could be the best one-two goaltending punch in hockey," Emile said. "The league has gone from six to fourteen teams, and the schedule from 70 games to 80 games. You travel coast to coast, more than 80,000 miles a year, and play as many as seven games in twelve nights. You can't expect one man to handle all your goalkeeping anymore."

Eddie didn't want to give up playing time, but once he started to get to know me, after a while, he was perfect with me. He agreed with the system; it gave him a chance to rest for the playoffs and it didn't hurt him—he played very well and won the Vezina for fewest goals-against in the league.

I think it made him last a couple of more years in the league, and we were the best of friends.

At the beginning, it was tough because I knew he didn't want me around because he played all those years by himself. He thought I was trying to get his job, which was a hundred percent wrong. But after a while, we were roommates, we used

Eddie Giacomin and I teamed up in goal for the Rangers and won the Vezina Trophy in 1970–71. (Gilles Villemure)

to go out all the time for dinner and things like that on the road, and we got along very well.

The quotes you read below came from an article Hugh Delano wrote in the Ranger program back then. He started that story by recalling a bus ride we had taken.

"Who's making all that noise up front?" asked Brad Park. "The goalies are at it again," said Rod Gilbert. Added Vic Hadfield: "Just a couple of old ladies who can't stop talking."

Said Emile: "Goalkeepers are like that. Always talking to each other. Comparing notes about different forwards and teams around the league and how they played, or think they should have played, a certain shot.

"Eddie and Gilles are always talking shop. Just like business partners."

And we were business partners who had paid off huge dividends for the business. In that same story, Emile said, "There's no doubt in my mind that the play of Eddie and Gilles was the biggest factor in our success." The other players used to call us "The Goaltenders' Union."

Eddie said: "I guess Emile knew what he was doing. Right? Not playing every game and getting the occasional rest helped me. I felt much stronger physically and mentally when we went into the playoffs. I felt sharper, more relaxed, and I found it easier to concentrate."

When it was my turn in net, Eddie would always cheer for me. He was there to help me with the players and their moves because he knew them all. That helped me a great deal.

"I guess we know better than anyone how much pressure there is for a goaltender. So we pull for each other," Eddie said.

"When I'm on the bench and Gilles is in trouble, I wish I could go out there and help him make a save."

When I was asked about our situation and people's comments that we didn't get along, I answered, "Eddie and I are teammates, not rivals. I ask Eddie a lot about shooters around the league since he knows them so well. He's a big help to me. We always try to perk each other up before games, regardless of who's playing."

In five years together, we never had an argument. We were close right after we got over that stuff at the beginning.

And we won that trophy. That year, I played in 34 games and Eddie in 46. We had a well-disciplined team. My goals-against average that year was 2.29. But I almost blew the damn thing.

There were two games left in the regular season (the awards are for regular season games), and we had a 10-goal advantage on Montreal for best average. The next to last game of the season was in Montreal and we lost, 7–2, with me in goal. This made me feel terrible, because our lead was down to five goals. But Eddie played our last game of the regular season and we won, 6–0. What a relief! Eddie and the guys came through. We won the Vezina—at the top of our profession.

Eddie, who had played all 70 games in each of the two previous seasons, had a 2.16 goals-against and eight shutouts. I had four shutouts, and the 12 by us combined was the most by a Ranger since a guy named John Roach had 13 in 1928–29 (heck, even I wasn't born then).

Another thing about Misters Giacomin and Villemure as a team: we were named to the All-Star team in both 1971 and 1973—the only goaltending pair from the same team ever to make the All-Star Game. And we did it twice. That makes me as proud as anything.

I was traded to Chicago on October 28, 1975. Eddie went to Detroit on waivers three days later. I saw recently where Rod Gilbert, talking on a chat on the Rangers' website, said, "It was a very sad moment. I think it was telling us that anyone could be traded, and it made me realize that hockey was a business."

As luck would have it, Eddie's first game with Detroit was back at the Garden. It was a very emotional night. Eddie was welcomed back like a returning hero. He beat the Rangers, and Wayne Dillon even said he was sorry when he scored on Eddie.

There was no reason to feel sorry for Ed Giacomin. He's a Hall of Famer. His No. 1 is hanging in the rafters at the Garden, along with the numbers of the other Rangers greats. Eddie had 54 shutouts in the National Hockey League and was as responsible as anyone for making the Rangers a viable franchise on the ice. He'll always have his place in Rangers history and in my heart. I loved my time with Ed Giacomin.

When he got traded, it was clear that they were breaking up the old gang, and Eddie went along with it. Things weren't going well and upper management decided it was time for a change, the big deal with the Bruins coming just a week or so later.

One of the strangest things that happened after the trade was a game I played against Eddie in Chicago. He was with the Red Wings and I was playing for the Blackhawks. He was at one end of the rink and I was at the other. He was looking at me, I was looking at him. We didn't know how to act. We're making signs at each other on the ice like, "How ya doin'?" That was fun.

I can't remember who won. They probably did because they had a good team then, but I don't remember the final score. But it was fun—he was looking at me and I was waving at him. It was a very strange night for both of us and made it sink home even more that those glory days with the Rangers were actually behind us.

Coming Close

I'd like to talk about our Rangers team between 1970 and 1975, a great group of guys, and a great leader who came very close to winning the Stanley Cup and who may have had the greatest Rangers team of all time.

Eddie Giacomin and I shared the goaltending, and we were a strong duo. Eddie played most of the playoff games. In front of us, we had a great bunch of guys.

We had a terrific power play with Brad Park, Rod Gilbert, Jean Ratelle, Vic Hadfield, and Bobby Rousseau, etc. We had a couple of penalty killing units—Walter Tkaczuk and Billy Fairbairn were the best in the business at that, and we had Peter Stemkowski and Bruce MacGregor also killing up front. Rod Seiling, Jim Neilson, and Dale Rolfe were also among those joining Park on the blueline. We always had strong defensemen and we had a great coach in Emile Francis.

Eddie and I played our game, but the players in front of us and Emile made our job so much easier. The system was so good that we had strong punch as well as defensive skill. And we had guys who cared about what they did. We used to have an optional skate at 11:00 a.m. the day of the game, and everybody would show up. Later on, when things started going downhill and

The most frustrating part about not winning the Stanley Cup was not winning it for head coach Emile Francis, who gave us his all. (New York Rangers)

after many of our players had signed big contracts that kept them from going to the new World Hockey Association, people called us "The Cat's Fat Cats," but other things kept us from winning the Stanley Cup. In my humble opinion, the effort was always there.

We were a family. Every time we went on the road, the whole team would stick together. We'd stop for a few beers and some food and spend all our time together. It was truly a special group.

Why didn't we win?

We had two years in a row there when we had the best, but guys got hurt. Dale Rolfe got hurt and Jean Ratelle got hurt. Goaltender Bernie Parent beat us in one series—he was unbelievable; he just stood on his head when we had a heck of a team. I think we had the best team the Rangers ever had, but we didn't win it because of injuries and goaltending that beat us. It was not because Eddie didn't play well. Eddie was outstanding, but Parent, he had 40-something shots in the seventh game I think. What can I tell you?

Triple OT

On April 29, 1971, the New York Rangers played one of the greatest games in the history of the franchise. I'd have to say it was the greatest game ever that I *didn't* play in.

I was on the bench that night. It was the sixth game of the series and one that could have put us into the Stanley Cup finals. We had beaten the Toronto Maple Leafs in six games in the opening round and were engaged in a truly classic series with the Chicago Blackhawks—Bobby Hull, Stan Mikita, Tony Esposito, etc.

We won the first game of the series in Chicago when Peter Stemkowski scored at 1:37 of overtime. It seesawed through four games before Hull's OT goal gave them a 3–2 lead. Then came Game 6—which I think will forever be known as "Game 6" in the hearts of Rangers fans.

They were beating us, 2–0, but Rod Gilbert scored in the second period, and Jean Ratelle in the third, and we tied the game. What happened next was not to be believed.

We played through the first overtime and into the second. In the second overtime, Stan Mikita, a Hall of Famer and one of the greatest ever to play the game, had an open net—an open, open net. Bill White's shot from the point beat Eddie Giacomin and hit the post and came right out to Mikita. He had the puck on his stick, he shot and hit the goalpost. It could have and should have been over right there. Instead, there was Stan, my future teammate and friend, draped over the top of the net after the whistle blew. He couldn't believe what happened to him. I couldn't either. "I should have just slid it in," said Mikita, who scored exactly 600 times in his long and proud NHL career. It should have been 601.

No one in the building could believe it. It was like the play happened in slow motion. We were supposed to be dead and then, suddenly, we weren't. And we would live to play another game.

We were alive, and Stemmer scored in the third overtime. We had just killed a penalty, and Tim Horton dumped the puck into the Chicago end. Teddy Irvine shot it from a bad angle, and Stemmer pushed home a rebound from just in front of Esposito at 1:29 of the third OT. The place went nuts. On the radio, Bill Chadwick, the Hall of Fame referee who was one of our announcers, yelled, "This team is gonna be tough to beat in Chicago on Sunday."

Well, we lost in Chicago on Sunday on a fluky goal that I think hit Cliff Koroll in the seat of the pants and dropped in. The final was 4–2, and the Blackhawks went on to lose to Montreal in seven games in the finals. Our Vezina Trophy season had ended, but not before the Rangers won the longest game the franchise had played in 33 years and at least avoided being eliminated on home ice. The fans went home happy. We were sleepy—-it was midnight—but happy.

The G-A-G Line

The name, supplied by Rangers statistician Art Friedman, stood for Goal A Game—which is what the line of Jean Ratelle, Rod Gilbert, and Vic Hadfield produced at the very least.

The line, which I think was the best in the National Hockey League at the time and maybe ever, really exploded during my first two years in New York. Ratty and Rod were responsible for the finesse, and Hadfield was one of the toughest guys in the league, one of the best at digging the puck out of corners. He also had a great shot. The line, sometimes also called the T-A-G (for two goals a game), was also the cornerstone of our strong power play, which had Brad Park and Bobby Rousseau at the points.

Rod Gilbert is still the Rangers' all-time leading scorer. You can also still make the argument that he's the greatest Ranger of all time.

Think about it—at one time Eddie Giacomin's No. 1 and Rod Gilbert's No. 7 were the only Rangers numbers up in the rafters.

Rod was very, very good. He had a good centerman, Jean Ratelle. I played junior with them. Oh, the passes were unbelievable. Jean used to set up plays and Rod would put it in. That was easy. You never saw the left wing—the left wing had to hang back. He would still score 20 goals, but those guys would work the offensive magic; they had the puck all the time, and that's why they played so well in the NHL for 15 years—they knew each other so well.

Rod had an incredible shot, but he needed Jean. Jean was the passer and set him up.

Off the ice, they were a little bit different. Jean was very quiet, but Rod used to go with the boys, have a beer, have something to eat. But Jean, after one or two, that was it for him and then he was gone. We had a good bunch of guys that liked to stay out. We didn't make a lot of money, but we had fun.

Anyway, I said the left wing skating with them just had to hang back and worry about defense. But in the 1971–72 season, Vic Hadfield, their left wing, became the first Ranger ever to score 50 goals in a season. He finished that off with two goals in the final regular season game, and that feat ranked right up there for us as a team with the Vezina Trophy I had shared with Eddie the previous year.

Any time someone from some group of guys does something, it's a team honor. We all felt a part of what Vic and the line were able to do. Eddie and myself were also happy we didn't have to face them—except in practice, where it only counted when we played shootout games after practice had ended.

Check the Rangers record books. Rod Gilbert is No. 1 in points, with 1,021, the only player ever to score 1,000 points in a Rangers uniform. Jean Ratelle is third with 817, while Vic

Hadfield is ninth at 572. Gilbert is first in goals, second in assists, and third in games; Ratelle is second in goals and third in assists; and Hadfield is fifth in goals and 10th in assists.

No. 7, No. 19, and No. 11. The G-A-G line. I never played with one any better.

The 1972 Finals

In 1972, we went to the Stanley Cup finals and faced the Boston Bruins—two outstanding teams against each other, both featuring outstanding players. The days when these two old franchises were at the bottom of the National Hockey League were long gone. The Bruins had won the Cup a few years earlier, and the Rangers were clearly ready—heck, it had been since 1940, so there was no time like the present. But, if you're reading this, chances are you know we didn't win the series.

Outstanding players? Boston had Bobby Orr, the greatest player ever to play the game, in my humble opinion. The Bruins had Esposito, Bucyk, and Hodge, and Cheevers in goal. We had Gilbert, Park, Vickers, Hadfield, Seiling, and Neilson, and Eddie Giacomin in goal, along with that Villemure guy. But we came into the series without Jean Ratelle, who would make it back for the finals but certainly wasn't the player who dominated for so much of the season.

We lost the finals, four games to two.

Eddie played the first four games. In the fifth game, he started, but he got hurt in the second period. The score was 2–2. Emile Francis put me in for the third period. I hadn't played for awhile, but, boy, I was ready to go. We won the

Jean Ratelle was the key centerman on the G-A-G line. (New York Rangers)

game, 3–2, in the Boston Garden. I stopped 18 shots in that third period. Bobby Rousseau, who had taken Ratelle's place after Ratty got hurt, scored the winning goal. The world was expecting us to go away quietly in that game, but we won and forced a Game 6 back at our place.

I guess because I played well in that last period, Emile put me back in goal for Game 6, at home. We lost, 3–0. I didn't play poorly, but Gerry Cheevers was better. We couldn't beat him. He stopped everything, and Orr was his usual magical self, clearly the star of the game as they avoided a trip back to Boston for Game 7 (with us having won 5 and 6 and captured the momentum). Mr. Orr beat us—he's just like a quarterback, that guy. And Cheevers was just too good.

Let me tell you, it wasn't easy sitting in the locker room while the Boston Bruins skated around the Madison Square Garden ice—*our* ice—with the Stanley Cup, knowing we had come so close after a very special season. I never had that experience before—to play the last game of the year. It was something. It was an experience.

We lost in six, but you can go back to Game 1 to see how the Bruins took control of the series. What a wild game that was. We had a layoff and came out flat and saw them take a 5–1 lead. Our wakeup call arrived in time and we stormed back to tie it, 5–5, in the third period. Then, Ace Bailey, never known for his scoring, broke around Brad Park and beat Eddie for the winning goal.

It was one of the two playoff goals Bailey scored in 10 years in the league.

Ace Bailey died in the September 11 tragedy. He was remembered in Boston and throughout the hockey world. I read an article in the *Boston Globe* that revealed Bailey wasn't even supposed to be on the ice when he scored that goal—again, bad luck beating the Rangers in a big game.

"I had told Ace specifically not to go on the ice, because I didn't think he was checking that well," Tom Johnson, his coach that day, said in the article. "Then somebody came off and nobody went on—there was a little miscommunication. So Ace jumps on, goes around Park, and scores the winning goal. I told him later, 'This is a secret between you and me.'"

Funny, years later, the Bruins lost a playoff series to Montreal when they had too many men on the ice. Here they may have won the Stanley Cup because they didn't have enough. Strange how things work sometimes.

Anyway, Phil Esposito said in that story: "I remember that goal like it was yesterday [So do we, Phil]. I can still see it, see Ace going around Brad Park. That goal turned the series around, and I told him that."

There was always something to keep us from getting to the promised land.

Bobby Orr

Rod Gilbert was once doing one of those online chats on the Rangers website and was talking about our trip to the Stanley Cup finals in 1972.

"I think that the two teams were equally balanced, except for possibly the one player that made the difference . . . what's his name . . . No. 4 for Boston? Oh, the great Bobby Orr. He made the difference out there."

Bobby Orr made the difference in every hockey game he ever played in. I have never seen a player control a game the way he did, which is why I think he's the best ever to play the game.

Years ago, in the 1950s and 1960s, a defenseman was strictly defensively minded. They never carried the puck. They passed it all the time, and they couldn't pinch inside the other team's blue line. Bobby Orr changed all that.

He carried the puck all over the ice. He pinched all the time, carried it deep, had the speed to get back, had a terrific shot, and won scoring titles. He made his teammates better hockey players by passing them the puck at the right time, right place. Just be in position; you'll get the puck. Just let him go where he wants to go, because he was all over the ice with

Here I am shaking hands with Bobby Orr, who was the difference in the 1972 Stanley Cup finals. (Gilles Villemure)

it, and just get ready. Phil Esposito, in one game against me, with Bobby Orr on the point, had 15 shots. He was in the slot and Bobby just passed him the puck—he didn't have to do anything. He had Ken Hodge in the corners and Johnny Bucyk in the corners, but Bobby was controlling the whole game. And as soon as he went up the ice, he was back.

He was the greatest ever—because of all the things he could do on the ice. It's just too bad he got hurt and had bad knees. But he was the best. He won the scoring title with 50 goals, 70, 80, 90 assists, Stanley Cup winner, Most Valuable Player in the league, great guy.

I remember one time I was playing against him in Boston, he fell on top of me. He says, "Gilly, are you all right, are you all right?" He was worried I was hurt, for Pete's sake. I said

I was okay and went back to his defensive position. Imagine that, how nice he was—usually a guy will punch you down again to keep you down.

Comparing Orr to some of the other greats I saw, Bobby Hull only had one dimension: shoot the puck. It was shot hard and went in, but Orr had 20 dimensions; he used to do everything from defensive skill to offensive skill. I wish I could name you a quarterback that would be outstanding, that would run the whole game, not only passing, but killing the clock and things like that, because quarterbacks could do that. He was the same way.

Lemieux and Gretzky only have one dimension, too—offensive skill. These guys were outstanding, you have to give them credit. And Gordie Howe was a tough guy, with a good shot, but Bobby had more. He was doing everything else, killing penalties—if you would give him the puck when you were a man short, he would kill the two minutes all by himself.

I once played an All-Star Game with Bobby Orr at the Boston Garden, his home rink. The other team shot the puck into our zone and I stopped it. Instead of giving the puck to Orr, I shot it around the boards. Well, the Boston fans got on me. Bobby was their man and they were 100 percent right! He was the best and I should have just given him the puck.

I played with Bobby in Chicago, and I had the chance to talk to him. He was as fine a gentleman as he was a hockey player. I was by myself in Chicago, and we used to go for lunch after practice, and he was there every day with the boys, one of us. I can't say enough about this guy. If he reads this book, he'll know who I am, because I had a good time with him.

Bobby's career numbers? How about 915 points in 657 regular season games and another 92 in 74 playoff contests? Think about that, a defenseman! Also think about what would have happened if he had two good knees. There's only one Bobby Orr.

 **Rangers Trivia #3**

Which of the "original six" has never been a Rangers foe in the Stanley Cup finals?

4

A Little Help from My Friends
Eddie Giacomin

"First of all, when I was twenty-six years old, stepping on Madison Square Garden ice, to me, that was an accomplishment in itself because that was my dream I'd always looked forward to. But then to go on and be fortunate enough to win the Vezina Trophy with Gilles Villemure, that became a reality, and here I am. Now, we've won something, and now my name is inscribed in that, and they can't take that away. And then, for me later on, to be inducted into the Hall of Fame, it shows you don't have to be a Stanley Cup winner in order to make that, and I do remember when I accepted the Hall of Fame that I accepted on behalf of all my teammates who are not going to be as fortunate as I am.

Emile Francis took a chance with a young goalie named Eddie Giacomin, and came up big. (New York Rangers)

"But the thing that hurts me the most is seeing that Stanley Cup when Boston beat us that sixth game at Madison Square Garden, 3–0, and seeing that Cup being paraded around. I had visions of wanting to charge and grab that Cup and take off. It was so frustrating because you've played all those years and that's as close as you're ever going to come to it. Not being able to manhandle that thing was very, very frustrating, not only for me but for many players. You don't get that opportunity, and there are tons of teams that never get the opportunity and we did have the opportunity. We weren't fortunate enough to win it.

"We never seemed to go into the finals, or any of the playoffs, at one hundred percent. We were always struggling.

I always maintain, even today, that the healthiest team will end up winning. We never want to use that as an excuse for why we didn't win, but we know how bad the individual is—I mean, I can remember Brad Park, he could barely lace his skates on, but once you get out there, it's a whole different ballgame."

On the Giacomin-Villemure team:

"We complemented each other so well because I caught with my left hand and he caught with his right hand. Any time there was a game involved, and Gilles was playing, it took the opposing team quite a while to catch on, and then if I was playing the next night, it was vice versa."

On the closeness of this team:

"Because our time together spanned seven or eight years, there was always good continuity amongst everybody. You always have a few little cliques where three or four would go one way, but in the course of a year, we were always together somewhere along the line. Today in sports you don't see that and that was neat for us.

"When I first started with the Rangers, Harry Howell had carte blanche to go to Great Neck Country Club, and this guy, Jerry Wolk, told Harry, 'Whenever you want to bring the team here, be my guest.' He was the president of the club at the time. That's when we were practicing at Skateland in New Hyde Park, and we would go, I would say between sixteen and eighteen strong, over to Great Neck Country Club and they'd just love it when we came there. Bagels and lox, pitcher of beer, you name it, anything we wanted to order. Harry Howell would just sign the check, and all we had to do was compensate

Jerry Wolk with some free tickets to Ranger games, no big deal. And here we are, in a strictly Jewish club, and everybody's drinking this beer—they hardly even drink that stuff, and here we are drinking by the gallon. It was always great, whenever we wanted to have a team meeting.

"This team was always together. Even when I was living in Manhattan and most of the guys lived in Long Beach, we were always together. Sometimes, it led to some long nights, but I've always said that's sports, that's cameraderie. I'd go home and have to pay the price, but I always looked at it as part of the game, and I always enjoyed that. That's changed now."

On Emile Francis:

"Watching the NBA finals, and seeing how Shaq played for Phil Jackson, I kinda feel the same way about all the years I played for Emile. First of all, Emile gave me the opportunity. He brought me to New York, put his neck out, and traded all those players for me. Then, a couple of things didn't go well, but he still stuck up for me. After that, I always referred to him as my father. I would go through a pane of glass for that man.

"He had a vision. And in order for him to go to Providence, R.I. and give up five players for me—especially me coming in at twenty-six years old—he didn't know what he was getting involved with, but he had this vision he had to start from the goal out and prioritize his hockey team. He had a philosophy that if you had a good goaltender and strong centers then you'll end up with a pretty good team, and he did that. He ended up getting good centers and myself, and a couple

Eddie Giacomin's No. 1 is one of the first numbers the Rangers retired.
(New York Rangers)

of years later bringing in Gilles Villemure, and we became the dynamic duo playing in goal.

"He made the New York Rangers in the 10 years I was there. He tried so many times to bring in other coaches, but it never worked out and he always ended up going back to the bench. He was the only one who could coach that team.

"Emile knew how to handle Rod Gilbert. He knew how to handle Ed Giacomin. He knew how to handle Bruce Mac-Gregor. He handled everybody basically the same. He treated us with kid gloves and once we became part of him, we were like sons to him. He puts us up there on a special echelon— we were special people to him, and he was very, very special to us.

"He was a special man. I give him so much credit. He got us out of trouble; he was always fighting for us at Madison Square Garden because we only had 40 dates on the big Garden calendar. He fought corporations on behalf of this hockey team. He tried to get us an extra half-hour on the ice—whatever it took for his guys."

On coming back to play against the Rangers after going to Detroit:

"I go on record saying it's because of that game, and it's because of how the fans responded, that kind of really, really set the standard to the Board of Governors for my selection to the Hall of Fame. I didn't win the Stanley Cup. The majority of people that make it have won the Stanley Cup. I didn't, but it showed how popular I was and how the fans reacted to you, and I credit the fans an awful lot as one of the reasons I'm in the Hall of Fame."

On what he said to Derek Sanderson to trigger a huge playoff brawl at the Garden:

"All I said to him was, 'We're gonna get you.' That's it. Those were the only words. It was a stupid thing because it was a commercial, nothing going on, and he was standing at that faceoff circle, and I just decided I would skate right up to him. And, of course, Derek being Derek, he just played that to the hilt and said we had a bounty and everything like that. Jennings came out and said, 'If we're going to pay anybody to get someone, it's going to be Bobby Orr, it's not going to be Derek Sanderson.' But all I said was 'We're gonna get you,' and that was it. As soon as we dropped the puck, and they went into the corner, that's when all helter skelter broke out. But none of the players knew what I said. Nobody. Those were the only words I said, and it worked."

On his final playoff game with the Rangers:

"We were playing the Islanders and we were down 3–0 after two periods. Emile Francis yanks out Villemure and puts me in for the start of third period. First of all, I was pissed off because I wasn't playing and now I would be going into the third period with no warmup. Who comes down but Garry Howatt? I chase him all the way up to the blue line, and I wanted to fight with him. But he wouldn't have anything to do with it. I'm skating up and I'm swinging at him and everything. He wouldn't drop his gloves or anything. Later on, we tied up the game, 3–3, but then we lost in overtime right off the first shot—bang, in the net, game over, and that's when the Islanders started their regime."

On Bill White and Stan Mikita both hitting the post in the second overtime in 1971:

"[Mikita] had a couple of chances to end that game. I've always said the goalposts are part of the goaltender's equipment."

On facing Bobby Hull:

"The theory always goes that Gilles Villemure would get to play against Chicago the majority of the time when we were together, because, believe me, who the heck in their right mind would want to play against Bobby Hull, anyway? But then when playoffs came, I had no choice, I had to play—or at least that's the way it seemed like it went."

 **Rangers Trivia
#4**

When Eddie Giacomin and I won the Vezina Trophy in the 1971–72 season, it marked the second of the four times the Rangers have captured that honor. Dave Kerr won it in 1939. Who won it after us and in what years?

5

Teammates

Brad Park

Brad Park was one of the top five defensemen in the National Hockey League. He was always being compared to Bobby Orr, the greatest ever, and Denis Potvin of the rival Islanders.

Brad always had the green light from Emile Francis to move up on the play and be an offensive force, much the way Brian Leetch was for the Rangers since he got there.

Brad was up in the play all the time. He was good at it. He used to keep the puck in the other end all the time. He was just as good as Brian Leetch, and Brian Leetch was good at it—keep the puck in the zone and keep the pressure on. Outstanding. Brad kept the puck in there all the time—and

Brad Park was one of the top five defensemen in the National Hockey League when he played. (New York Rangers)

he only needed a foot or two to move the puck and do something with it. That's all Brad needed. That's how good he was with the stick.

Naturally, any time you have a defenseman taking chances on the offensive end, you face your share of two-on-ones against the goaltender. But we had Dale Rolfe and Jimmy Neilson—and sometimes Rod Seiling—on the left side, and they were always there to take care of things when Brad got trapped. Any one of those three guys knew how to play the odd-man rush perfectly. Whenever Eddie or myself was in goal, the defense would stay in the middle of the ice and play the pass. The only thing the goalie would have to worry about was a shot from a bad angle.

But Brad Park didn't get caught that much. And he was just a tremendous offensive player—and as tough as they came, too. He made our power play go, shifting over to the left side with Bobby Rousseau on the right.

Injuries hurt Brad during his days with the Rangers, days that ended with that shocking trade to Boston in 1975. But as soon as Park arrived in New York, he was a fan favorite. He had this face like a little boy, but he played like a lion. I remember one big story on him—I think it was in *The Sporting News*—and the headline read: "Ranger Rookie Amazes, Amuses Garden Fans." This kid was special. We played together in Buffalo, but he wasn't there long—17 games. He was quickly on his way to Manhattan, where he should have played his whole career.

As well as Emile Francis got along with his players, and he was always fair to us, Brad was a contract holdout in 1970 and missed the opening game. With the WHA looming,

The Cat wound up giving Brad the biggest contract in the league at that time. He was our captain when he was traded to Boston.

For his career, which ended in Detroit, Brad Park scored just over 1,000 points, counting playoffs. He's fourth on the Rangers' all-time defensemen scoring list, even though he scored more points after he left New York than he did with the Rangers.

Brad Park in a Boston uniform never really looked right or made sense, but he was able to continue his Hall of Fame career there and make all of us regret the day he was traded away. It's also a shame Brad never got to win that Stanley Cup, even playing for some very good Boston teams after leaving us. But that can't do anything to diminish a brilliant NHL career for a great guy.

Bob Nevin

Bob Nevin was captain of the New York Rangers when I got to the National Hockey League on a full-time basis.

The fans didn't always appreciate Bobby and they booed him a lot. But what a hockey player. He had hockey sense.

Nevin never said anything, but I appreciated him. Every time I had the puck, I used to shoot the puck around the boards. I had two good guys for me—Billy Fairbairn and Bob Nevin. I didn't have to look; they were there. I've got the puck, guys are coming in, I shoot the puck around the boards to my right, and both those wingers would be there for me every time! On that side, I was covered. I didn't have to worry about anything. Ever.

Nevin was a good hockey player. I remember a goal he scored to eliminate Toronto in a playoff series in 1971, his last year with the Rangers. In Game 6 at 9:07 of the first overtime, the captain scored, the goal giving us the first playoff series win for the franchise in 21 years. I remember the shot because it stuck in the Toronto net and just stayed there. The series was over and Newy had left the winning goal stuck in the twines. Then we went on to that great seven-game series against Chicago where Pete Stemkowski scored two OT goals.

Nevin could score—he had 31 goals in a season twice in the NHL, once in Los Angeles after he got traded away, first to Minnesota for Bobby Rousseau and then on to L.A. (on waivers). He scored 307 goals in the National Hockey League, but he didn't have a big shot. He had skill.

The Rangers got him from Toronto in that big trade in 1964—the one that sent Andy Bathgate and Don McKenney to the Leafs and brought Nevin, Arnie Brown, and Rod Seiling to New York. You have to wonder if New York fans resented Nevin for replacing a popular guy like Bathgate, but Bob Nevin had a good career in New York and never let the fans bother him.

Slats

Dave Schultz and Glen Sather were both tough guys in the National Hockey League at the same time. Schultz, one of the proud leaders of the Philadelphia Flyers, the Broad Street Bullies, was bigger than Sather, the man we called "Slats," who would eventually wind up running the Rangers. I don't care about Schultz's size, though; no one was tougher than Slats and no one had a bigger heart.

So, the size thing didn't matter when these two guys hooked up. One night at the Garden, we were playing the Flyers, and it was always a night of action when those guys were in town. Good hockey, good goaltending, and there were a lot of superstars on both sides. And there was plenty of rough stuff and the Garden crowd was always into it in a big way. It was special when the Flyers and Rangers played at the Garden in those days.

On this one night, I happened to be near Schultz and Sather when a whistle blew, and they started to push each other. I hear Schultz say to Slats, "I have to prove myself in this league." He wasn't talking about scoring goals here; Schultz would score 79 goals in his NHL career. He was talking about fighting. Glen looks at him and says, "Well, let's go."

They dropped their gloves and went at it. It was one of the best fights I'd ever seen. Glen never backed off because Schultz was bigger. Glen earned my respect and the respect of his teammates right there. Tough guy, Glen Sather.

Sather, who went on to have all that success in Edmonton before moving back to New York, scored 80 goals (one more than Schultz) in an NHL career that saw him play in Boston, Pittsburgh, New York, St. Louis, Montreal, and Minnesota. But he has a small place in history for a goal he scored that doesn't count in any record book—he scored the first goal ever at the Nassau Coliseum when we played the Islanders in their first exhibition game there. Now, it's hard to believe, but the Islanders are in Brooklyn.

Walter Tkaczuk

Phil Esposito scored 778 goals in the National Hockey League, including playoffs. During the 1971–72 season, he had 66

Walter Tkaczuk held Phil Esposito scoreless in the 1971–72 Stanley Cup finals. (New York Rangers)

goals in the regular season and nine more in the playoffs, leading the league in both.

But when we played the Boston Bruins in the Stanley Cup finals, Espo was held scoreless. Six games, no goals, with Walter Tkaczuk the primary man checking the Bruins' big gun. No ordinary task, but Walter was no ordinary hockey player.

The following year, we knocked the Bruins out of the playoffs, and Walter was brilliant again. When that series was over, Derek Sanderson said, "He's New York's best center, better than Ratelle. You've got to put him right up there behind Phil Esposito. He's a superstar, but he just doesn't know it. He may be the best two-way player in hockey."

To which Emile Francis added: "He's what two-way hockey is all about."

Walter Tkaczuk—what a hockey player. He was strong and impossible to knock off his feet, and he had a career that was a great one with the Rangers and would have been better had it not been for injuries; the last, an eye problem that forced his retirement.

He was the most honest player on the ice. He could do everything. You couldn't hit him, couldn't put him down. I remember one time when he had his head down and somebody hit him. If it would have been somebody else, he would have been out. He just stood there and shook it off and kept on going.

He was a good defensive player, mostly a defensive player, and he and Billy Fairbairn were so great at killing penalties for us. They were unbelievable. Walter was a strong man. He didn't score too many goals, but he had so many skills and his line—the Bulldog Line, with Fairbairn on the right and first Dave Balon and then Steve Vickers on the left—was a perfect No. 2 line for us.

Walter suffered a broken jaw one year, was out two weeks with the jaw wired shut, lost a lot of weight, came back, and scored two goals in his first game. That night, The Cat said, "He's quite a guy. He's out for two weeks, can't eat or breathe properly, has a busted jaw, and comes back and pops two goals." Bep Guidolin, who was coaching the Bruins that night, said, "He's a remarkable hockey player."

He was. Said Walter after that game: "My pregame meal was two glasses of tomato juice, chicken soup and a milk shake."

Tkaczuk scored 246 goals, counting playoffs, in a 14-year career all spent with the Rangers. Through the end of the 2001–02 season, he was still fifth on the team's all-time scoring list, fifth in assists and games, and ninth in goals. No. 18 is truly one of the Ranger greats.

Bill Fairbairn

When people talk about Billy Fairbairn, they always say the same thing about him—he was a very hard worker who was willing to do anything to make his team win.

He was quiet, hard-nosed guy, and I always knew where Billy was in the defensive zone. If I had the puck and I had to shoot it at somebody, and he was on my right side, which was my forehand because I was a left-handed goalie, I just had to shoot it around the boards and he was there. One hundred percent of the time I could depend on him.

He and Walter Tkaczuk were great penalty killers. They were tireless. Billy didn't have the talent of a Rod Gilbert or anyone like that, but he was a defensive player and he did his job. And could he ever take a hit along the boards to make a play.

And he could score. Billy scored 175 goals in the NHL counting playoffs, so we can remember him as more than just a checker. No. 10 was a complete hockey player in my book.

Jim Neilson

"He stops shots. He clears the puck. What else can you ask of a defenseman?"

The words were spoken nearly thirty years ago. It was *me* talking about Jim Neilson, "The Chief" and a great defenseman.

In those days, Brad Park was one of the best defensemen in the game, but he was an offensive defenseman, and we had guys, Jim Neilson, Rod Seiling, and Dale Rolfe, there to back him up. Jimmy Neilson was a goaltender's best friend. I knew exactly what Jimmy would do in front of me, and he always knew what I was going to do.

He used to block shots and he didn't care if he got hurt. And he was a hell of a guy—he was quiet, did his job. He was kind of a joker, too, a hell of a guy. He wasn't flashy at all, a defensive defenseman. He was like my buddy back there.

Jimmy Neilson played almost 1,100 games in the National Hockey League, finishing his career in Calgary and Cleveland. He scored 70 goals, one in the playoffs. This guy was true defenseman and a real teammate.

*As a defenseman, Jim Neilson was a goaltender's best friend.
(New York Rangers)*

Steve Vickers

Steve Vickers is one of my friends you're hearing from in this book. And he was one of the toughest hockey players I ever played with.

Tough? Dave Schultz would have no part of him—no part. Steve asked him many times to go. They were both left wings. They would meet and Steve would say, "Any time you want, I'm here, man." Steve was tough.

If somebody did something to Walter, or Billy, or anyone on the ice, Steve was right there.

He could also score. Vickers replaced Dave Balon on the left side of the Bulldog Line with Walter Tkaczuk and Billy Fairbairn and eventually replaced Vic Hadfield on the GAG Line.

It was hard to move Steve away from his "office" in front of the net, and those guys were so good finding him there, and he was great putting away rebounds. I read once that Steve said, "Any dummy can stand by the post. It's getting the puck to go in that can be tough. Sometimes it does, sometimes it doesn't."

For Vickers, it went in 270 times in a career that lasted until 1981–82, and it was all with the Rangers. He joined us the year after we went to the finals but got to go with the team when they lost to the Canadiens in 1979.

The Captain

In the 1971–72 season, Vic Hadfield became the first New York Ranger to score 50 goals in one season. And he did it in style, scoring his 49th and 50th goals on the final day of the regular season.

Steve Vickers, part of the Bulldog Line, put in 270 goals in his career. (New York Rangers)

The game itself didn't mean anything. But we knew what the day was all about—Vic. It was on national television against the Montreal Canadiens, the team we would beat in the first round of the playoffs. We lost, 6–5, to extend our season-ending winless streak to six games. But Vic got his goals, and the place went crazy.

Vic was more than just a goal scorer. He was our captain after Bob Nevin left. He was a hard-nosed hockey player, and any time the game would get rough, he would take over. Vic would drop his gloves against anyone. He never scored more than 31 goals in any other NHL season, and never more than 28 in any other year with the Rangers, but everything worked for him as the left wing on the GAG line that one year.

They were the best line in the league, and Vic was the protector of the other two. The Rangers weren't known for being that tough in those days, but no one was tougher than Vic Hadfield.

For his career with the Rangers and Pittsburgh Penguins, Vic, No. 11, scored 323 goals and had 389 assists. He also had 1,154 penalty minutes in 1,002 games, scored 27 goals, and had 117 penalty minutes in 73 career playoff games. Quite a guy, Vic Hadfield.

Stemmer

Pete Stemkowski was probably the funniest guy I ever played with.

We called him "The Stemmer," and he became known for scoring that triple-overtime goal against Chicago in 1971. We knew him as much more than that.

Pete Stemkowski was probably the funniest guy I ever played with. (New York Rangers)

During practice, Stemmer would shoot the puck at my head. He thought this was a riot. I would skate back after him and try to shoot the puck back at him. Emile Francis would be in shock. He didn't know what to think watching this little goalie skating after one of his centers. The bottom line was that Stemmer never hit me and everything was in fun.

He was also one of the greatest joke tellers. Before games, we would come in from the warmups and the guys would be all keyed up for the game. Everything would be quiet in the dressing room, and then along came Stemmer. He had a way of making the guys relax and taking the pressure off by telling jokes or firing one-liners. He kept everybody alive. You were down in the dressing room, we lost a couple of games in a row, and Stemmer would stand up and tell a few jokes before the game, after the game, *during* the game—he was that kind of guy. Wide open all the time. Never down. He was funny.

I remember in Boston during the fifth game of the 1972 Stanley Cup finals, that after the second period, the score was tied, 2–2. If we lost, we would go home and the Bruins would win the Cup. Eddie had gotten hurt and I was going to play the third period. The dressing room at the Garden was quiet, and then along comes this one voice—Stemmer. He said, "Guys, if we lose, we're playing golf tomorrow." Well, we went out for the third period and won the game, 3–2.

Stemmer didn't have enough magic words for the next game, though—the Bruins beat us 3–0 and skated around the Madison Square Garden ice with the Stanley Cup.

We got Stemmer from Detroit for Larry Brown on Halloween 1970, my first full year with the Rangers. I knew what kind of hockey player he was, a big, strong guy, good on faceoffs, and a great defensive player who turned us into an even better defensive hockey club, but I didn't know what kind of guy he was in the locker room.

You need somebody like him in the locker room to loosen everybody up because there can be a lot of pressure all the time. They talk about trades and things like that, and you've got a guy like him to perk everybody up. You need that, and he was it.

Stemmer finished his NHL career in 1978 after playing one year for the Los Angeles Kings following his release by John Ferguson (he also played 24 games for Springfield of the AHL in 1978–79). He played in 887 regular season games, scoring 193 goals—never more than 25 in a season—and adding 331 assists. In the playoffs, he had 53 points in

81 games, including TWO overtime winners in that series against Chicago. Stemmer now teams in Ranger history with Don Raleigh (the 1950 finals against Detroit) and Stephane Matteau (the '94 semis against the New Jersey Devils) as the only three Rangers to score two overtime goals in the same playoff series.

One more thing about Stemmer that people tend to forget about—he came up with Toronto and was part of one of the biggest trades in the history of the NHL. On March 3, 1968, the Maple Leafs traded Frank Mahovlich, Garry Unger, Stemmer, and the rights to Carl Brewer to the Detroit Red Wings for Norm Ullman, Paul Henderson, and Floyd Smith. Pretty big names right there.

Mahovlich and Ullman are in the Hall of Fame. Henderson scored that famous goal for Team Canada against the Russians in 1972. And Unger became the iron-man cornerstone of the St. Louis Blues for all those years.

If you're going to make a trade, you might as well make it a big one, like the one Emile Francis and Harry Sinden shocked the world with in 1975.

Tim Horton

My first full year in the NHL was also Tim Horton's only full season with the Rangers. The future Hall of Famer came up in 1951 with the Maple Leafs, and the Rangers got him from Toronto for the stretch run of the 1969–70 season. Look at his record—the guy had 10 seasons in which he played all 70 games for the Leafs and one where he played 74.

He fit in well with our team—he was a monster. He was the greatest—I roomed with him. A big guy, he used to wrestle with you. Forget about it—he'd put you down in a second, that's how strong he was. What a great guy he was! He would do anything for you.

When he died in a car accident, you had that surprised feeling because you thought he was too strong for anything like that to kill him. And he was doing very well—he had Tim Horton's Donuts back home and he was doing very well for himself. They have those in some places in the States now, but in Canada it's huge. He was a great guy.

Terry Sawchuk

Before I finally joined the Rangers for good, Emile Francis had problems finding the right backup to Eddie Giacomin. The Cat knew Eddie was playing too much but just couldn't come up with the right answer for the backup. The last one before me was future Hall of Famer Terry Sawchuk, who was there for 1969–70 (I was at Buffalo again that year) but only played in six games. One of those saw him record the 103rd shutout of his distinguished career.

I roomed with him. He was at the end of his playing days. Great guy. He was teaching me how to play because I thought he was one of the greatest ever: Sawchuk and Johnny Bower. I learned a lot from him.

Sawchuk was 3–1–2 with a 2.91 goals-against average in eight regular season games for the Rangers and lost his only playoff decision. He died during the off-season after an incident with another teammate, Ron Stewart, who later became my last Rangers coach. I don't know what happened, but it was ruled an accident. But knowing Sawchuk for the time I did helped me a lot in my hockey career.

The All-Time Leader

Rod Gilbert made an interesting comment the night he passed Andy Bathgate and became the Rangers' all-time leading scorer with 730 points.

"Johnny and Vic will probably score 1,000 before me," he said that night. "They're much stronger guys than me."

At the time, Johnny (Jean Ratelle) had 685 points. Vic Hadfield had 730. Neither got to 1,000 before Gilbert, who still stands as the only Ranger ever to score 1,000 points in his Rangers career.

All three have their place in Rangers history. What a line! But Gilbert was the big-name guy, the guy made for New York City. He's still there and is still working for the Rangers.

Ron Greschner

One of the greatest Rangers ever is a guy you don't always hear a lot about: Ron Greschner.

Think about it—Gresch played 982 games in the National Hockey League, all with the New York Rangers. That's fourth on the team's all-time list. He is seventh on the Rangers' all-time scoring list and is also second in points, goals, and assists by Rangers defensemen, second to Brian Leetch in all three. He played forward later in his career.

Gresch, the picture of smoothness and stickhandling, came up to the Rangers for the 1974–75 season, as a nineteen year-old kid, and it was clear right away that he was something special—just the way he carried himself on the ice.

One of the important factors in any team's defensive system is communication between the goaltender and his defense. Ronnie was always willing to listen and learn. Whatever I said, he did. He lasted 16 years in the National Hockey League, so I guess I didn't hurt him.

Only Harry Howell and Rod Gilbert played more seasons with the Rangers.

Gresch, who hailed from the great town of Goodsoil, Saskatchewan, battled through terrible back problems and became one of the great Rangers. He was a great guy.

I read quotes in the *Rangers Encyclopedia* produced by this company years back that showed what Gresch had to say about the great city of New York—interesting comments for a kid from a small town in western Canada. Late in his career, Gresch, who married supermodel Carol Alt, said, "I think anybody who says something negative about New York doesn't deserve to play here. It's a fascinating city; there's always something going on."

Ron Greschner scored 179 goals and 610 points in 982 regular season games, and another 17 goals and 49 points in 84 playoff games. All of his numbers would have been greater had it not been for the back trouble that limited an outstanding career.

Ron Harris

Ron Harris was a tough defenseman on our team who scored only 24 goals in over 500 National Hockey League games,

Rod Gilbert still stands as the only Ranger ever to score 1,000 points in his Rangers career. (New York Rangers)

counting playoffs, in a career that also included stops in Detroit, Oakland, and Atlanta. But three of those goals came in the same playoff year, 1974, and one of those was a crucial overtime winner in Montreal.

The series was tied, 2–2, and the fifth game was up there. We were down, 2–1, late in the game and pulled Eddie Giacomin for a sixth skater in the final minute. Bruce MacGregor, who scored our first goal, tied it with 16 seconds left in regulation. In the overtime, Peter Stemkowski won a faceoff from Peter Mahovlich in the Montreal zone and got the puck to Harry, who was playing right wing in the game. He one-timed the puck past Bunny Larocque; we won the game and went on to win the series, and they were the defending Stanley Cup champions. We then lost to Philadelphia in seven games, and they went on to win the Cup.

Anyway, here's the thing about the Harris goal. "I told my wife if there was an overtime, I was going to score the winning goal," Harry said after the game. Imagine that, a guy who never scored. She must have thought he was crazy. Turns out he wasn't that crazy.

In another playoff, Harry took Phil Esposito out with a clean hip check and knocked him out of the series with a knee injury. Espo knew it—if you cross the blue line, and you've got your head down, Ronnie's going to get you. It was a clean check, which is what he usually threw.

Years ago, there used to be hip checks at the blue line all the time. There was Ronnie, and Bobby Baun, from Toronto, and Leo Boivin. Brad Park was good at it, too. You used to go right over the boards if you weren't careful.

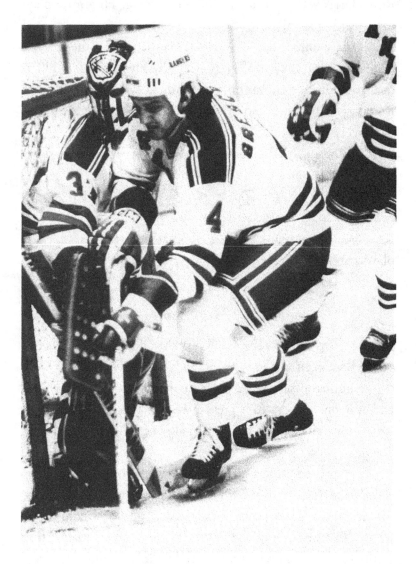

Ron Greschner played 982 games in the NHL—all with the New York Rangers. (New York Rangers)

Ron Harris was good at it and very strong. He didn't play dirty. Strong man!

I know one time, in Philadelphia, he was on the ice, on his back, and one of the big guys on the Flyers, Dave Schultz or Gary Dornhoefer, was on top of him and fighting him, and Ron was on his back and beat the heck out of the guy, on his back! Very strong.

One more thing about the Espo hit by Harris—Phil wound up in the hospital with knee surgery, and his teammates wound up kidnapping him from the hospital in his bed and taking him down Causeway Street in the bed to the team's season-ending party. I guess that's just the way hockey players are.

Rick Middleton

I couldn't believe it when the Rangers traded Rick Middleton to the Boston Bruins for Kenny Hodge on May 26, 1976.

Middleton scored 22 goals his first year, 24 his second, and was on his way to a great National Hockey League career that would see him finish with almost 500 goals, counting playoffs.

He proved how good he was with Boston, and they called him "Nifty," but I always liked him. He could do so many things, was a good skater, had good hands and great talent. This was one of the first deals the Rangers made after Emile Francis was fired and replaced by John Ferguson. Fergy figured Hodge, who was Phil Esposito's right wing in Boston, would help Espo adjust to New York. The trade was a disaster for the Rangers.

You could tell Middleton was going to be a good hockey player. His hands were unbelievable. He wasn't a big guy, but could he play!

Some people say he got traded out of New York because of the night life, and that may well be true. But once he got to Boston, just like Brad Park, his career took off. He had 38 goals his second year with the Bruins, and it was already clear by that time the Rangers had made a big mistake.

Career numbers? He had 448 goals (as many as 51 in a season) and 988 points (a high of 105) in 1,005 regular season games and added 45 goals and 100 points in 114 playoff games. Any time you average almost a point a game in your National Hockey League career, you are a great player. He's also third on the Bruins' all-time goal-scoring list, fourth in points, and sixth in assists.

Hodge scored 21 goals for the Rangers in 1976–77 and two in 1977–78, and his career was over. Middleton played until 1988. Nice trade, guys.

Ted Irvine

On February 28, 1970, Emile Francis traded Juha Widing and Real Lemieux to the Los Angeles Kings for Ted Irvine, a tough left winger who had gone to the Kings from the Bruins in the expansion draft. Irvine would become a solid player for the Rangers before moving on to St. Louis in the 1975 trade that brought John Davidson to the Rangers.

After getting Irvine, The Cat said, "We need some muscle. I saw him in the playoffs [when he scored five goals in 11 games] when he got into a dragout brawl with Bob Plager. That

Plager's a pretty tough guy in a fight. Teddy more than held his own. That sold me on him. Right then and there I knew I wanted him."

Irvine scored 20 goals in his first full year with the Rangers (also my first full year) and later had 26 in a season. He had 170 goals, counting playoffs, in an 11-year NHL career.

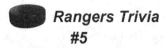 **Rangers Trivia**
    #5

Who holds the Rangers record for playoff games played?

6

A Little Help from My Friends
Rod Gilbert

"Gilles comes from Three Rivers, and I come from Montreal. We met, actually, in Guelph, Ontario—three little French Canadians out of the water, basically trying to learn how to speak English. There was not that much of it where we came from—Ratelle, Gilles, and myself.

"We had this really, really tough coach named Eddie Bush. He was really something. His job was to try to discourage the kids to see if they had enough guts to survive all his nonsense. His teachings were very different from anybody else's. He used to beat up on guys; he used to fight in the locker room with some of the players, wrestle them down, and call them gutless.

Rod Gilbert and I played junior hockey together in Guelph, Ontario. (New York Rangers)

It was quite interesting, but we all survived it. Then Ratelle came up here before me—I had a serious injury when I was nineteen and took a year off. Gilles wound up in Buffalo with Fred Shero.

"In those years they didn't believe in the two-goalie system. A lot of the teams only had one goalie who was so superior to the other one—they wouldn't spend the money to secure a second-string goalie. Our team, having Eddie Giacomin, Emile Francis's protege because he had given seven players to acquire him, it was very difficult for Gilles to break in here. Had he been with another team, I think Gilles would have been a superstar, because I think he was equal to Giacomin in ability to stop the puck. But Eddie was here, Eddie was flamboyant, and he could handle the puck like another defenseman out there and made it to the Hall of Fame, and he could display his ability because he was playing the majority of the games. But if Gilles had played as many games as Eddie, he would have been as successful, for sure—so you could see the combo of the two of them playing for us, the one year we were invincible with those two guys.

"Gilles was a very sound, cool goaltender—he didn't get excited. The position of goaltending probably requires more than any other position as far as not being jumpy, because you make a wrong move and the puck is behind you. Gilles was settled all the time, played his angles, and was a student of the game. He was the hardest for me to score against in practice. We used to have these bets, and I'll tell you what, he beat me a lot."

On the change from losers to winners:

"It was basically Emile Francis's doing by transforming the team into a younger team. I was really sad when I got here, and I got to play three years with Andy Bathgate, when they traded him to Toronto along with Don McKenney. I was kind of apprehensive about that. He was my mentor; I was learning a lot from him, and I guess Emile Francis decided it was time to rebuild the team, and he got Rod Seiling and Arnie Brown and Bobby Nevin and Bill Collins, young players. They came here, and I think it was the beginning of the ascension.

"Getting Gilles to come up here with Eddie Giacomin was another major move. Then, of course, we had two of the best players who played for the Rangers. Brad Park, who went to the Hall of Fame, was on defense, and he was rated not far behind Bobby Orr, and then you had Walter Tkaczuk. And then Emile complemented the team with Pete Stemkowski and Teddy Irvine, Bruce MacGregor, and Davey Balon. I think we jelled quite well together. He kept the team as a group for a number of years. We all had the same common goal, and it was fun.

"Why we didn't win? There's only one team that wins at the end, and the reason we couldn't beat Boston in 1972 was mainly because of Bobby Orr."

On this group being close:

"We were extremely tight. We all lived in the same area, Long Beach. Emile Francis had this about him—he made sure that everyone on the team was treated the same way, whether it was Vic Hadfield or Gillies Villemure. Everybody was the same. His philosophy was you're only as strong as your weakest link, so, therefore, if the last three or four guys, the guys who didn't get as much ice time, didn't feel as much part of the team as I did, he felt the team wasn't going to be successful."

*Dave Balon (above), formed the "Bulldog Line" alongside Walt
Tkaczuk and Bill Fairbairn. (New York Rangers)*

How crazy was Pete Stemkowski?

"Stemmer was wonderful. He was a practical joker, and he had all these one-liners. He enjoyed life to the fullest. He used to keep the team loose. He remembered everything, and he saw the humor sometimes in very serious moments. He saw the humor of it, and he used to use it and keep the team loose.

"I used to dress well, and every time he'd see me with a new suit and stuff, he'd say, 'Hey Rocky, nice suit—who shines it for ya?' He used to get me all the time.

"Stemmer was a very special individual."

On a French-Canadian kid falling in love with Manhattan:

"When I was nineteen and twenty, I stayed on here with Emile Francis and Harry Howell to do hockey camps at the old Madison Square Garden. I met all the kids that were coming to the camp, and I met their parents. So now the parents are enjoying what I'm doing for their kids, and they're treating me to the best restaurants in Manhattan, taking me to Broadway plays, taking me to Wingfoot in Westchester to play golf, and I kind of enjoyed that. I developed some strong relationships and friendships, and that was it."

On having his number retired at the Garden:

"That's a big honor. You think about all the players—[and I'm glad that they've added more—guys like Andy Bathgate and Harry Howell]. Certainly, Brad Park made a big contribution here.

"When the kids go there, they can relate to me now. I try to help them. I go to after-school programs and take them to the Garden and I think that's one of the things that impresses them the most. 'Oh, they retired your number and it's hanging there at Madison Square Garden, it's wonderful! Wow!'"

On almost becoming coach of the Rangers:

"I left the Rangers for a while to open a restaurant and work on Wall Street. I was a little disappointed. Sonny Werblin, rest his soul, had promised me the coaching job, and I went to New Haven to coach for one year, rode the buses, and prepared myself. He had asked me to coach the Rangers, and I told him I wasn't ready yet, but I asked him to promise me that I could go down there for a year and then come back up and coach the Rangers. I said, 'That's the only team I want to coach—I don't want to move out of New York.' He promised me I would get the job.

"I did my apprenticeship at New Haven and gave a course at Yale, and I did pretty well, made the playoffs, and then I was ready to come up here. Fred Shero was leaving, so the position was open, but I didn't hear from Werblin after the season. So I stormed into his office and said, 'Why aren't you returning my call or why aren't you talking to me—we have a deal.' He said, 'Well, did you like it down there?' I said, 'I liked it, but it's over—I'm ready to take over the Rangers.' He's squirming, he's not even looking at me and he says, 'Well, you know the success of the Olympic Team in Lake Placid . . .' I said, 'No, you didn't, did you?' He hired Herb Brooks. I said, 'How many years?' He said, 'Four years.' I said, 'Well, I wish you well, I wish the Rangers well, but here's my resignation, and you can't count on me for anything around here anymore.' I was angry."

On coming back to help the Alumni Association:

"In 1989, Steve Vickers and Bill Chadwick were very active, and I helped them, but not as much as I'm helping now. It has grown tremendously. But the problem with the area of New York is there's not that many players that live here. I can count on Gilles, but we used to have Pierre Larouche and Marcel Dionne and Ulf Nilsson; all these guys left. Now we just have a few guys. But we do things; we have a golf tournament, and we raise money, and we have the Man of the Year, and we bring the guys in. We're still active, we keep in touch with a lot of them and try to help them in any way we can.

"Most of the guys are doing well. There's not that many requests. We helped Davey Balon, he had MS, but all in all, I think the majority of the guys are doing pretty well. Some could do better, but that's confidential, of course."

On the breaking up of the team, and adjusting to life with Phil Esposito, hardly his best friend:

"It was very difficult, I'm sure it had some effect on me. It wasn't only Espo. The loss of Brad, my closest friend, with Ratelle, my roommate who I've known since I was ten years old, and Vic Hadfield on my left side—those were my bread and butter. We had a tremendous amount of success together and as a team. You sort of expect something—I had gone through Andy Bathgate, so nothing surprised me. I had seen the greats get traded from the Montreal Canadiens. Think about Jacques Plante and Doug Harvey coming to the Rangers, and I had the pleasure to play with them. I knew there was always that possibility that things would change, but I didn't think Emile Francis was going to be put in that situation to make those moves. I think he was forced to do it, by this guy Michael Burke, who has passed away.

"It must have been more difficult for Emile because those were his protégés, and he had built this, and to see it disintegrate like that . . . and then the fact they brought Ferguson here to team up with Espo, and Espo becoming the captain ahead of Walter Tkaczuk or myself just didn't make any sense.

"It was a different team, let's put it that way. It was a different era, it was a different Rangers and life goes on. I was very affected by it. I was sad and depressed at times. I have a pretty strong will to accept a lot of conditions. It wasn't death, it wasn't sickness, it was just an organization that was trying to survive."

On rooming with Ratelle the day of the trade:

"Jean is a very unemotional person to start with. They were all in a state of shock. I remember them sitting on their suitcases. I don't think it was handled very well. They were just told, coldly, but I remember them just being beyond belief. They didn't expect that. I don't remember much; I probably chose to block it out. Ratelle was very nondemonstrative. It was almost like the news turned into anger and inward silence. It wasn't until we played in Boston (the following month) that I got to share with him a little bit of his feelings.

"They both went on and did well. They're true professional players, and the reason this took place was Harry Sinden. He had Jean, Brad, and myself on Team Canada, and we were successful in Russia. All three of us played the four games in Russia, and Brad and Jean were tremendous. Sinden was our coach, so he knew the quality of these two guys. He just pulled the trigger and that was their gain. Getting Vadnais and Esposito here didn't change too much, but the worst trade was Rick Middleton for Hodge. Those consequences were very serious.

"Phil did well when he came here, and Carol held his own. But for Ferguson to trade Rick Middleton—that's gotta go into the Rangers' history as the worst. I think Ricky led the Bruins for 10 years. Ferguson caught him one night, I think he was off guard somewhere with maybe a few drinks, but you know where it came from, it came from Esposito. He wanted Hodge. Imagine if Esposito didn't want something? You give a twenty-one-year-old kid who was a wizard on the ice—why would you give him up for a thirty-two-year-old guy? Does that make sense to you?"

On being there for the Cup in 1994:

"That was the most incredible experience. I had been really close to that team that year. I started with them in London, England, when they went there to play a couple of exhibition games against Toronto. I got to travel with them and got to know Mark Messier and Brian and Beukeboom and all those guys. It's just like all the pieces were falling together, and it was almost like, 'Could it be? Could it be?' I went to Vancouver for the sixth game, and I was really hurt. We should have lost 10–2 there. We got beat up real bad and then we're coming back here for the seventh game. I had to shoot a commercial that afternoon for Prodigy, and I think I had a little bit of a stroke in the middle of my shoulder blades, I was so nervous. I couldn't even read the teleprompter, I was that nervous.

"When we scored the two goals at the beginning of the game, I relaxed a little bit. Then there was celebration."

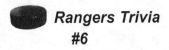

Rangers Trivia #6

Brian Leetch has had six of the top eight point-scoring seasons by a Rangers defenseman—Nos. 1, 3, 4, 6, 7, and 8. Who are the other two who cracked that list?

7

Derek Sanderson

Toward the end of my days with the Rangers, we picked Derek Sanderson from the rival Bruins. Derek scored 25 goals for us his first year in New York, where he was perfect for the lifestyle.

Good hockey player, good guy, Derek Sanderson. He was outspoken, and the media was after him all the time. He had all his stories. I'll never forget that he was the first one nearest the door in the dressing room and all the media was there. Nineteen other guys, no problem, there was nobody around. They wanted Derek. He had that personality. He was a natural with the media. He got all the attention. We didn't have to say anything because they all wanted to talk to him.

He was making big money, and he was a good hockey player. Off the ice, he was a little wild. He was a young guy with money in New York. That can be a dangerous combination.

We heard stories about his past, how the Bruins would leave for road trips and Derek would park his car in front of Logan Airport, just leave it there. It would be towed, and he'd come home from the trip and bail his car out. They got to know him at the impound lot. He didn't care about the money—he had tons of it because of the World Hockey Association, where he only played eight games but got a lot of money up front. That's the way he was in those days. He had a good time.

When he was with the Bruins, he was a pain. We had a big brawl with them in the playoffs one year that started with Eddie skating out and saying something to him. Derek was always instigating, and those Bruins teams had a lot of guys who could help back him up. But he was a tough guy, a pest, and a great, great penalty killer and defensive player. That team was known for the Orrs, the Espositos, and the Bucyks, but Derek, Eddie Westfall, and Don Marcotte were great checkers and penalty killers.

We traded Walt McKechnie to the Bruins to get Derek, who never played much with Boston after his WHA experience. He played only one full season with the Rangers and was also gone from New York the same week Emile traded me and Eddie just before the big deal with the Bruins. Derek was traded to St. Louis and scored 24 goals there the rest of the year, actually finishing the season with a career-high 67 points, all in the 65 games with the Blues after he went scoreless in eight games with the Rangers.

For his career, Derek played 13 seasons and had 202 goals. He wound up doing a lot of broadcasting with the Bruins. Great guy.

No one will ever forget Derek Sanderson's rather brief stay with the New York Rangers. He was a special kind of guy, and everyone seems to have a Derek Sanderson story.

Says Peter Stemkowski: "He was a beauty. Derek was the kind of a guy that if you got him in a group, Derek had to be the center, and Derek had to tell a story, and Derek could top anything that you had. But you got Derek one-on-one, he was a good guy.

"I always remember the cute story about Derek Sanderson. He lived in Manhattan and practiced in Long Beach. I guess he woke up and missed his ride out to the Island. I remember a hundred stories about Derek Sanderson, but this one comes to mind. I guess he was in Manhattan, his ride was supposed to pick him up and honked and honked, but I guess he was late getting out of bed so the guy took off, and he ended up taking a cab from Manhattan to Long Beach. He got to Long Beach, and it was like sixty, seventy bucks—whatever it was—and Derek didn't have the cash.

"So he came in the locker room, and here's this little guy, the cab driver, typical cab driver—the Danny DeVito look, with the cap, and I guess Derek said, 'Well, I don't have the cash, but just park here and I'm gonna go in and get some money off the guys in the locker room.' He walks in the locker room, and here's this little guy following him. Now, we pick up on what's going on, right? So, Derek said, 'Hey, I need sixty bucks to pay this guy,' so we were all like, 'Aw, payday's next week, I don't have it.' We were like really breaking his horns here for about fifteen minutes. He needed sixty bucks to pay this guy; this poor cab driver was going from stall to stall.

"I said, 'Derek, I got four bucks on me, I didn't bring my wallet.' Polis caught on and said, 'Derek, I don't have it.' We just let him hang there for about ten, fifteen minutes, then he finally got the money and gave it to the guy. That was Derek Sanderson. You never knew what to expect from this guy."

More Derek

Stemmer continues with the Derek Sanderson stories.

"He was something else. He got a lot of money from the WHA, but that wasn't his role. Derek was a good role guy third-line, penalty killer. You can't take Derek Sanderson and say, 'Derek, you're going to be my Wayne Gretzky, you're going to be my main man, you're our leader.' Derek's not a leader. Never was a leader. He made a lot of money, spent a lot of money.

"There are so many Derek Sanderson stories. I remember when he was here and Rick Middleton was playing with us. I guess he called up Rick Middleton right after the season and said, 'Rick, I'm gonna pick you up in about fifteen minutes.' Derek had this limousine kind of thing—I don't know what he was driving, a Jaguar or whatever he's driving.

"Rick said okay, Derek picked up Rick Middleton, they got in the car and Rick asked, 'Well, where we going?'

"Derek said, 'We're going golfing.' Rick said, 'Derek, I don't have any of my stuff here. Why didn't you tell me we were going golfing?'

"Derek said, 'Don't worry about it.' I guess they pulled up to the golf course, they go right to the pro shop, and he said to him, 'What do you like? Grab a set of clubs and grab a pair of shoes, and that's it.' I guess Derek had the gold American Express card at that time, picked something out, shoot, I don't know, three, four hundred bucks, threw the card on the table, paid for it, and they went and played golf.

"Golf was over, they got in the car, headed home, and I guess Rick Middleton said, 'Hey, hold it—I think I left my shoes and my clubs back there against the fence, left them for the guy to clean off when we went to get something to eat.' Derek says, 'Nah, forget about it,' left the clubs back there and that was it. That's the way Derek lived.

"Derek would throw the card down. Derek would take his buddies to Hawaii, throw a gold American Express down. Bob Wolff was his agent, and Wolff would get these bills at the end of the month, 25, 30 thousand dollars. He went to Hawaii, took five friends, flew first class, United. That was Derek [laugh].

"I only spent a year with him, but, boy, there's more things that that guy did . . . he lived in Manhattan. He wasn't going to live in Long Beach, that's for sure. He liked the lights. I don't know what he did away from the rink, because I was out here and he was there, but he got along with everybody. There was no one who didn't like him. You just put up with him and just kinda shook your head at the way he was."

And Even More Derek

Rod Gilbert chimes in with the following Derek Sanderson story:

"I recall Derek coming to the Rangers, and we would always go out after practice and after games we'd stay in town and go to il Vagabondo, this old Italian restaurant on the east side. On the road, Brad and myself and Vic and Glen Sather we were always together.

"I recall being at this place and having to share the bill. I think there was six or eight of us together. It didn't come to too much—maybe ten dollars apiece, and Derek Sanderson was brand new, and he said, 'You guys are so cheap, let me pick up the bill.'

"I said, 'No, Derek, just put your ten dollars in the middle of the table there.'

"So he had one hundred dollars out, and he wanted to give it to the waitress.

"I said, 'No, just put the money in because we all share.'

"So he took a lighter and lit the hundred-dollar bill on fire. We all watched him burn it, and none of us stopped him.

"He was really upset. Then, after he burned it, I said, 'Okay, now put the ten in.' That was to tell him we all share."

Eddie Giacomin, who was there, recalls it differently. He says Derek burned *two* hundred dollar bills, not one. "Dale Rolfe was there," Eddie says, "and he turned to Derek and said, 'You say you have a lot of money, watch that sucker *burn!*' The first one went, and the waitress was right there, and her eyes just went crazy—that was a hundred dollars—and he turned around and lit the second one, of course with the intention of putting it out, but Dale Rolfe grabbed his wrist and said, 'Watch that sucker burn.'

 **Rangers Trivia
#7**

*Before winning the Stanley Cup in 1994, the Rangers'
last visit to the finals was in 1979, when they lost
to the Montreal Canadiens. Can you name the three
teams the Rangers beat to get to the finals that year?*

8

A Little Help from My Friends
Brad Park

"My first two years in New York we were just in the transition of really going into a two-man system [of goalkeepers]—the first year, Don Simmons was the second goaltender, the next year it was Terry Sawchuk. Unfortunately, Terry passed away. I played a little bit with Gilles in Buffalo before I got called up in '68. He was an impressive goaltender, and they went on to win the Calder Cup that year. Then, they brought him back up. We saw him in training camp, and then he was up a little bit if Eddie got hurt. It wasn't really until he came up after that, and you're seeing him every day in practice, and the first thing that hits you in practice—and this is my third or fourth year in the

Brad Park was an All-Star six seasons in a row for the Rangers, from 1969–70 through 1974–75. (New York Rangers)

league—is you can't beat this guy. Probably the best angle goaltender that I've ever seen—his angles and his quickness were impeccable. You started to appreciate the things he could do. Also, handling the puck—he probably didn't shoot it as well as Eddie Giacomin, but handled it in tight very well. He was basically a good standup goaltender. I think in practice is when it really started to sink in what a great player he was.

"When I saw him in Buffalo, he had a great attitude because he was the consummate professional. He worked every day, he played all the games, he played hard all the time. So when you looked at him, even though he was down there, he never really took a day off. He didn't look forward to day off. [His attitude] was, 'This is my job, this is how I do it and I'm going to do it the best I can.' I believe he was out to prove a point that if the Rangers weren't going to use him, somebody else would. He was out there to impress other people."

On being part of a team that won the Vezina Trophy in front of Giacomin and Villemure in 1970–71:

"Emile Francis had always prided himself and made the team have pride in their defensive game. He set goals for us to keep the goals-against under 200. The year that we went with Gilles and Eddie, and Gilles was getting more games in, it was a nice fit. Between him and Eddie, they had a common goal, and that was for the team to win, regardless of who was in net, there was no jealousy on either part—whoever was in net we were going to play for him and he was going to play for us. That was a great attitude and that was just a fun attitude. There was no pettiness involved. The success of the team is what really mattered, and it started in the goal and moved out to your defensemen, and we, as defensemen, were more than happy to play in front of these guys."

On the goalies having competition with the other players:

"They would challenge us all the time in their own way. Eddie was much more vocal in his challenge in practice when you were shooting on him—probably much more of an extrovert than Gilles. But Gilles would very quietly say, 'Hey, I own you.' We used to do shootouts and things like that, and they were always challenging us, as well as each other, and that was very successful. We played shootout for money after practice with Gilles and Eddie, and if you got two out of five on breakaways, you won. After I got traded to Boston, three of five, you won. These guys in New York were that confident. They knew you and what you did, and they challenged you. They had to stop four out of five to win, and that's how highly they thought of themselves."

On Peter Stemkowski:

"Stemmer was a beauty. They don't make them like Stemmer anymore. Stemmer was a character. Every day he was the lively voice in the dressing room. A lot of the humor came from Stemmer, the fun times. He could break guys' chops in a fun way without hurting them."

On the Rangers being perhaps the best team that never won a Stanley Cup:

"I think it was probably the best and the closest, yeah."

On the chances of that 1971–72 team winning the Cup if Jean Ratelle didn't break his ankle:

"Pretty good chance, yeah. He was having a banner year, and when a guy has a banner year, it carries right into the playoffs."

On his fondest memories of his Rangers years:

"Probably the way we hung out together. It didn't matter what age you were, if you were thirty or you were twenty, nobody was ever excluded. On the ice, I guess one of the most satisfying things was the year after we lost in the finals to the Bruins, and the next year we went back and we beat the Bruins in Boston. There was a great deal of satisfaction there because that rivalry was so strong."

On switching sides in that rivalry after The Trade in 1975:

"It wasn't my fault. It was a shock. I had kinda moved along, I had been in the organization for seven years and moved up to where I was the captain. Getting to that point, I was Ranger blue through and through and to go to Boston was such a shock to my system, especially to my nervous system. I cried. I was very disappointed and very upset when that happened. I remember calling my wife, and I had to hang up on her because I couldn't talk to her anymore. But I went to a very stable organization, and the Rangers got very unstable."

On Emile Francis:

"I think a great deal of the man, even though he traded me. I think a great deal of him because he was honest, he expected you to play, expected you to participate. He was appreciative of the way you went about your job. The guy, in management, he was the consummate professional."

On criticism of the team after players signed big contracts not to go to the WHA. Many said the Rangers were soft:

"I don't believe that. I think we were fighting two things— we were fighting a little bit of age and we were fighting a little bit of toughness. Philadelphia came in after that, and they changed the way the game would be played, and that was difficult. There was a whole new set of rules coming in. Philadelphia came in as the Broad Street Bullies and initiated a lot of physical play, a lot of fights, things like that, and that was a whole new concept we hadn't seen. We ended up playing that seven-game series against them in 1974. We had more points than them, and they had the home-ice advantage, and I think that hurt us a little bit [the Rangers lost Game 7, 4–3, and the Flyers won the Stanley Cup]. But we were still a strong team. The two-out-of-three series, which was kind of a fluke, against the Islanders, that dictated, a little bit I'll bet, the dispersal of that team and that kind of brotherhood.

"It kinda started in the summer when we traded Jerry Butler, Teddy Irvine, and Bert Wilson to St. Louis for John Davidson and Billy Collins, and that was a lot of character off that team. Then we got into training camp, and in October, Derek Sanderson was off to St. Louis, Giacomin was waived, which was an unbelievable situation that he would go on waivers. [The night] he came back was probably the only game we ever threw. We threw that game, we can say we didn't, but we did.

"This was a dispersal of that team. I think if you talk to Emile, basically Gulf & Western told him to get rid of the high-priced guys who were not producing. I believe he went to Bill Jennings and didn't get any support from him. He knew his days were numbered. I think Harry Sinden in Boston had inside knowledge, and the reason I say that is that Ratty and I played for Team Canada in '72 and he knew what kind of people we were, how we practiced, and how we played."

 **Rangers Trivia #8**

In 2001–2002, Brian Leetch became the third player to play in 1,000 regular season games as a Ranger, moving into third place on the club's all-time list at 1,021. Harry Howell (1,160) is the leader, followed by Rod Gilbert (1,065). Who is next on the list, sitting in fourth place?

9

Breaking Up Is Hard to Do

There were a lot of people who thought the Rangers became soft after the money came in and players started to get paid more because of the World Hockey Association being there to try to steal players away. We used to see people calling the Rangers "The Cat's (Emile Francis) Fat Cats." I don't agree with that label.

Even though we didn't win the Stanley Cup, we still played well for a year or so. I don't know what happened after that; just before they traded everybody, we went flat! The whole team went flat. For what reason, I don't know. I never found out why. It just happened, and it sadly led to the end of our days together in New York.

But soon after that, they started trading everybody and began breaking up a great team that just never managed to win it all. It should have ended better than the way it did, with all of us taking our memories to different cities around the National Hockey League. We all knew this was a business, but when you're as close as we were as a team, it's tough to see it all end—one of the toughest things that ever happened to me in the game.

Traded

I never could really imagine not being a New York Ranger, or at least part of the only organization I ever knew. But after we lost a first-round playoff series to the Islanders in 1975, it became more and more apparent that the gang wasn't going to stay together much longer. I decided to tell Emile Francis something I never imagined myself ever saying.

I asked Emile to trade me. Nothing was working; I hadn't played in a game to that point, and I told him, "If you can get somebody for me, then go ahead and do it." The next day, I was gone, off to Chicago for defenseman Doug Jarrett.

The whole team was getting traded—upper management traded everybody because it just wasn't working anymore. Derek Sanderson was traded the same day I was; Eddie Giacomin went three days later, and then came the big deal with the Bruins in which Brad Park and Jean Ratelle were swapped for Phil Esposito and Carol Vadnais, a deal that fans of both teams will never forget.

Not long after, Emile Francis was gone, too, and a wonderful era of the New York Rangers came to an official end.

When I finally did get to Chicago, it felt very strange putting on that sweater. Very strange. What a weird feeling—when

When I was traded to the Chicago Blackhawks in 1975, it felt very strange putting on that sweater. (Gilles Villemure)

they took a picture of me, I couldn't believe it. Oh my God! I got scared. Really. From sixteen until thirty-five years old, I'm a Ranger. All of sudden, I'm not any more—I'm going to Chicago now. I'm divorced; I'm by myself.

I didn't know anybody on the team, but those guys were great. Dennis Hull, Stan Mikita, Tony Esposito, they used to invite me over to their homes all the time. But there were two French guys, Alain Daigle and J. P. Bordeleau, who were there and helped me a lot. Alain Daigle came from my hometown, which also helped. He was a young kid; he was twenty-two years old, I think.

I played quite a few games my first year with the Blackhawks. My second year, I broke my finger twice and didn't play that much. Then it was time for me to retire. I could tell that the reflexes weren't there anymore. I was getting slower, and the puck looked a little smaller. That's the truth—guys used to shoot from the blue line, and I'd say, "What the heck, I can't see it." Time to quit and that was it. I had had enough.

Wheeling and Dealing

I was traded to Chicago on October 28, 1975. Derek Sanderson was shipped to St. Louis two days later and Eddie Giacomin was off to Detroit a day after that. But this was all just a prelude to what would happen only a week later.

Talking years later, Emile Francis told my coauthor, Mike Shalin, how "The Trade" came about. Emile and Harry [Sinden] were talking about trading 13th players for 13th players, and Emile finally just said, "Let's do something big." Something big? The Rangers traded Brad Park and Jean Ratelle to the Bruins for Phil Esposito, Carol Vadnais, and a defenseman named Joe Zanussi, who always called himself "The Fifth Wheel."

What a trade! Three Hall of Famers, Park and Espo, and Ratty, one of the greatest players ever to wear the Ranger uniform. Fans in both cities were in shock. But it was starting to become clear, in New York anyway, that it was time for a changing of the guard. We had lost to the Islanders in the first round of the playoffs the year before, and Emile was crushed by that. It was clear the great years of the Rangers, at least *those* great years, were over.

A little background. The Cat dealt Ted Irvine, Jerry Butler, and Bert Wilson to St. Louis after the previous season for a young goalie named John Davidson and Bill Collins. The overhaul was under way. Ron Stewart, our old defensive specialist during his playing days, was the new coach. Then came the two goalies' move and "The Trade" with the Bruins.

The Bruins were in Vancouver when the trade was made. Later on, in his 75th anniversary book about the Rangers, John Halligan wrote that Bruins executive Nate Greenburg said Sinden received death threats after making the deal. Wayne Cashman, Espo's left wing in Boston, was so upset he threw the television set through the window of his Vancouver hotel room, and it went crashing to the street below. Halligan also wrote that Cashman ordered 100 sandwiches from room service and charged them to the Bruins.

It was truly the end of an era in both cities. The hated rivals had essentially swapped their heart and soul to each other. Fans in both cities were confused and didn't know how to act. Park had ripped the Bruins heavily in a book he had written, and Rangers fans hated Esposito.

But it all worked out. Park and Ratelle became stars in Boston, Espo wound up taking over the Rangers after his playing days ended, and that young goalie, Davidson, took the Rangers to the Stanley Cup finals in 1979. Emile was fired soon after "The Trade," but his hockey career wasn't over—he still had work to do with the St. Louis Blues and Hartford Whalers.

One more thing about "The Trade": when Espo came to the Rangers, Rod Gilbert was still there, and he was No. 7, the same number Phil wore in Boston. Phil first wore No. 5, Dale Rolfe s old number, with the Rangers, then switched to No. 12 (Ron Stewart's), before finally settling in as No. 77.

Stan Mikita

When I think about the colorful people I played with in the National Hockey League, Derek Sanderson's name comes to mind. But Derek was kind of in his own world when we played together with the Rangers—he was a young guy with a lot of money, so he didn't hang around with the rest of us too much.

When I think of funny guys, I keep coming back to Peter Stemkowski and another guy I played with in Chicago, Stan Mikita. He was funny.

Somebody told me before I went to Chicago, "He's an asshole; he's not a nice guy," but when I got there, it was a completely different story. The guy was great for me—*great!* He and his wife were unbelievable—I was over at his house all the time. "Come on, Gilly, we'll go for dinner." On the road it was the same way. And what I heard before that, before I got there, was "This guy ain't nothing." I couldn't believe how good this guy was. And I'd say he was a character.

We used to go to races together. I was single then, and many nights I was by myself, and he'd say, "C'mon, let's go, we're going out for dinner." And he was one of the great players. He was a great player—tough, chippy, but a good hockey player, a Hall of Famer. One year he was a tough guy, and the next he won the Lady Byng Trophy for gentlemanly conduct, because he wanted to show he could do it. That's the kind of guy he was—whatever he wanted to do, he did, except score against us with the open net in New York in the second overtime in 1971.

He was a good hockey player, though—over 1,600 points in his career, including playoffs. I had the chance to play against Stan Mikita and was glad to get the opportunity to finish my career with No. 21 on my team.

Hull of a Shot

Hockey fans today enjoyed watching Brett Hull star in the National Hockey League all those years. And Hull was a great offensive player. In my day I got to face his father, the great Bobby Hull, the Golden Jet, and his uncle, Dennis.

Some people felt Dennis actually shot the puck *harder* than Bobby, even though Bobby had the reputation. But Dennis had a different shot; Dennis had a hard time controlling where the puck was going. It was fast. He broke my finger once in practice. I went to catch the puck, and you have the stick against your finger, and, boom, I broke it.

What I remember about Bobby Hull is he took a slap shot on me from the blue line—years ago they used to have that big curved stick, before they really clamped down on them. Well, Bobby took a shot from the blue line, and the puck was waist high. All of a sudden, it was a foot off the ice and went right through my legs. I'll never forget that.

Another thing I remember about Bobby Hull is that he used to take a slap shot while he was skating. He's going a hundred miles an hour, and all of a sudden the big swing. And he used to come down the wing all the time—like outside the faceoff circle to my right. The goaltender has no place to go now—you have to stay there and face the wrath of that shot. You don't have much of the net covered, and he's coming in there so fast, and you can't move. That could get very scary because you had no place to hide. And I had my glove on my right hand, which made it tough because he had more of the wide side to shoot at it. It really was an intimidating thing. You knew he wouldn't pass it, so you just had to get ready for it the best way you could.

He had the hardest shot I ever saw—he and this one guy who hurt me, a guy from Philly, Reggie Leach. He hurt me. I tried to catch it, and he had a heavy shot. I used to catch the puck away from the webbing, on the outside, so a hard shot could hurt me.

We had a guy who came up to the Rangers who could fire the puck—a defenseman named Larry Sacharuk. But no one shot it harder than Bobby Hull.

The thing about the great shooters was that it was no different to play them than it was to play anyone else. You knew they were going to score more, that's all. You couldn't let them intimidate you, because that could get inside your head and cost you your focus. One lapse in focus can cost you a hockey game.

For their careers, the brothers wound up with over 1,000 goals against innocent goalies like me, counting playoffs. Toss in the 800 or so that Brett, the "Golden Brett," has scored, and you have, if I can say it, a *"Hull* of a family." Sorry about that.

My Style

When I was traded to the Chicago Blackhawks in 1975, I became the backup for future Hall of Fame goaltender Tony Esposito. I had some things in common with Tony—we were both wily veterans, and we both caught with our right hands, which is unusual for goaltenders. But our similarities really ended there—on the ice, anyway.

Our styles were different. I was a stand-up, angle goaltender. Tony was a flopper, playing the style the kids are playing now, butterfly style. But he was good at it, very good. There were not too many like him. Most of the goaltenders in those days stood up; Jacques Plante, Terry Sawchuk, Johnny Bower—he would never fall down. Never. And I was the same way I believe, because I was small, I had to stand up, or they would have killed me on top. I lasted 20 years doing it, 20 years of pro hockey.

Nowadays, it's a different style. They all play the butterfly style. Some of them are good at it, some of them are not (it's like anything else, I guess). Tony was good at it—maybe the best ever. I guess that's why he's in the Hall of Fame along with his brother Phil.

I was always a stand-up, angle goaltender. (Gilles Villemure)

Tough Nights

One of the keys to being a successful goaltender in the National Hockey League is the ability to forget what happens in one game and go on to the next—especially when that previous game is a disaster. We all have them; we all have to recover.

I remember watching the playoffs and seeing Jose Theodore give up five goals on five shots to the Carolina Hurricanes in the deciding game of a playoff series. That's tough—here's a guy who carried his team into the eighth and final Eastern Conference playoff spot and then beat the No. 1 Boston Bruins in the first round of the playoffs. Then, his season has to end like this, he has to live with it all summer rather than being able to come right back in the next game—same thing happened to the great Patrick Roy. That's the life of a goaltender—but he has to tell himself, and others have to tell him all summer, that he was the main reason they got as far as they did. Sometimes, you can say the words, others can say them, too, but you're the one who gave up the goals.

I had many tough nights during my playing career. And even though this is a book about the New York Rangers, one of my worst came in Pittsburgh after I left the Rangers and was traded to the Chicago Blackhawks.

The score was 11–1, and I wouldn't be telling this story if we were winning. There were about three minutes left in the game, and I was not playing well, to say the least. They left me out there because they didn't want to bring Tony Esposito off the bench in a game he was supposed to be sitting out and resting. So, I was in there for the duration.

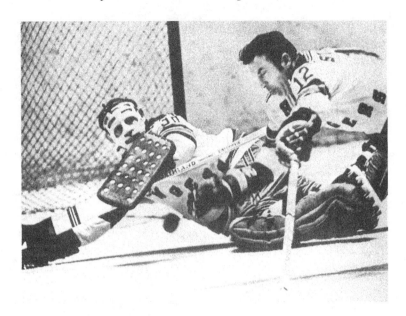

I couldn't stop every puck that came my way, especially one night after I left the Rangers and was playing for the Chicago Blackhawks. (Gilles Villemure)

After a whistle, I notice the linesman coming toward my net. What he was doing was checking the net to see if there were any holes in it. Linesmen do that from time to time during a break just to make sure the net is all right.

Well, the linesman was behind the net, and I was in front. I yelled to him to come to the front of the net, and when he came around, I said to him, "You see the big four-by-six-foot hole in front of the net? Would you repair it, please?"

I got a big laugh out of him.

I never let myself get too down after a bad game. There's always the next game to redeem yourself. And it's the same thing when you get a shutout—it means nothing once the next game starts, so you can't go out there thinking you're ready for the Hall of Fame. This can be a very humbling game, even if your name is Dominik Hasek or Patrick Roy.

 **Rangers Trivia
#9**

Two players share the Rangers record for fastest two goals by one player. Can you name the two Rangers who have scored goals eight seconds apart in the long and proud history of the team?

10

A Little Help from My Friends
Peter Stemkowski

"Back then, when Gilles was breaking in, there were six teams, twelve guys, and the backup really didn't play very much. Does anybody remember Glenn Hall's backup in the glory years, or Terry Sawhuck's backup? You don't remember these guys. Expansion helped a lot of guys.

"We had six teams up until 1967; we went to twelve, and that opened up some doors, and in the seventies, they expanded again, but at that time you did what you had to do. Nobody went to college or graduated or had something else to fall back on. Back in those days, you played hockey as a kid, and if you were good, you progressed into the juniors, you came, and you signed a pro contract. The money was like $5,500 the first year and maybe $6,000 the second year with a couple thousand signing bonus—that's what you were making and you just didn't know anything else.

"If you didn't play hockey what would you do? Nobody had any kind of a trade or anything like that. Now guys are coming out of Boston College and schools like that, and have something going, and if they turn pro now, they make so much darn money—a million bucks, and that can carry them the rest of their lives. I remember the year we won the Cup, I made $9,000—and I think we made like [another] six or seven [thousand, as a Cup share]."

On coming so close with the Rangers:

"Ratelle went down one year. That didn't help. We had the ingredients. We beat teams we shouldn't have beaten, and we lost to teams we shouldn't have lost to. Bobby Orr? That hurt, but what are you gonna do? It's like Peter Forsberg a while back, one of the greatest players, and he goes out and wins games. When Bobby Orr was on the ice and they beat us in six for the Cup, that was the year. I think we were at our peak then. Guys strarted getting a little old after that. And then that series against the Flyers—losing that . . . then we started to dismantle, then the pieces started to break off a little bit.

"That was some series. When I go back and think, I have never been involved in a best-of-seven series like that, even from a broadcaster's point, which is what I'm involved in now. That was a hell of a series, that one. We lost in seven, we got called for too many men on the ice by John D'Amico, we lost by a goal, we got one late in the third period—I think I scored it—and Hadfield was serving the penalty, and they caught him with a chuckle on his face in the penalty box. He was gone after that—Emile took exception to that. Then Hadfield went, and the team started to dismantle. We had Vic and Walter and Billy Fairbairn and Eddie and Villemure there—we had our team, we had our chances. I was there through the thick and thin, and then when John Ferguson came on the scene, he didn't really care much for me. He and I ran into each other quite a few times in my early going when he was with Montreal and I was with Toronto, and I don't think he ever forgave me for some of the run-ins we had. It was just the beginning of the end—they brought in Wayne Dillon and Pat Hickey and . . ."

On Villemure's contention that Stemkowski fired pucks at his head in practice:

"Yeah. Well, I didn't do it on purpose, but, occasionally, one would get away, and he'd chase me around the rink. Everybody would stop and say, 'Oh, ho-hum, there's Stemmer and Whitey going at it again.'

"I used to call him Whitey because guys used to come to training camp in the fall and at least spend an hour or two on the beach and get a little bit of color. But he was just white, and I asked him what he did in the off season—did he work in a flour mill, or what? So I nicknamed him Whitey, and I think we all called him Whitey after that. I still call him Whitey to this day.

"He never caught me. Listen, I was big; I wasn't the fastest guy, but I could out-skate him, a little short, stubby guy who played goal.

"We used to practice at New Hyde Park, and one would get away, and he'd get a little upset and chase me around the rink a couple of times and get back in the net and practice. Emile Francis would say something, and I'd say, 'Hey, it's not the first time it's happened, it won't be the last, so get it out of your system, Gilles, and let's get back to practice.' He says maybe it wasn't an accident when it happened, but you've got a puck, and you've got a stick, sometimes you've got a two-iron in your hand and keep it low and hit it off your back foot, and sometimes you've got a wedge in your hand and it kinda gets away on you. It always depended on which way the wind was blowing.

"New Hyde Park was quite a place. It had that chicken wire around the boards. It was cold, ice-cold. It wasn't exactly the spacious and beautiful practice facility that the guys have today. We used to walk downstairs, and I think we had nails to hang up our coats that were knocked into the wall. Now, you walk into the locker room and there are fifteen treadmills and twenty stationary bikes, a fitness guy—we never used to have that.

"It was nice when we moved to Long Beach because all the guys lived down here. A couple of guys lived in the city, like Bob Nevin and Rod Gilbert, and I think Eddie Giacomin ended up living in Manhattan, but we were all here on Long Beach. These were all summer rentals back then. It was ideal for us. I'm in Atlantic Beach now, right next door."

On Villemure saying Stemkowski is the funniest guy he ever played with:

"Really? That's quite a compliment. That's quite a reputation to have to live up to. I don't know how many funny things

I did. I used to do impersonations and things like that. Sometimes people tell me I did things that I don't even remember. I mean, Emile Francis says, the triple overtime goal, I walked into the locker room—I guess I must have said it—'The concessions have run out, bars are going to be closed, let's get this thing over with,' and lo and behold, I'm the guy who goes out and scores the winning goal, gets it over with so we all go home around midnight.

"Gilly was the kind of guy you could kid around with, call him short and Whitey, and he took a good ribbing. I was a kind of a jokester where I could poke nicknames at guys. Like, Gilles Marotte drove this small, little car and I called it the Batmobile and he kinda took exception to my calling it the Batmobile—it looked like the Batmobile—but with Villemure, you could kid around with him and he wouldn't mind. He always had trouble with the first shot on goal. I don't know what it was with him, but I'd say in the locker room, 'Jesus, Gil, let's get a beach ball and somebody shoot the damn beach ball, stop the first shot, then you're okay.' He had a tendency to always let the first shot in for some reason, I don't know why."

On winning that game with one of the biggest goals in Ranger history:

"Both teams were just running on fumes. You're at the point where nobody's any fresher or nobody's more tired than the other guy—you're all at just about the same level at that point. You're numb, actually, just numb, and you're just thinking, 'I don't want to make the mistake that's gonna cost this game.' Everybody was pretty cautious.

"I think [Tim] Horton dumped it in, and that was his last point as a New York Ranger. I just followed up the play. A lot of people think I was a slow guy getting in there last, and I tell people I was the first guy in, that's how I got to the puck. I just tucked it in the short side. Irvine took the shot, the puck was lying there, and I just put it in.

"I think we went to Gallagher's, across the street there, after the game, and we sat there until about two in the morning and I think I came out here to Long Beach, and there was a place that stayed open until about five o'clock; you couldn't sleep after something like that. I remember me and Dale Rolfe—he was rooming with me at the time—just stayed up until about six or seven o'clock in the morning, just sitting, talking, and nobody seemed to want to go home. I remember finally leaving this place, and there were kids getting on the school bus. I said, 'This is a bit strange—I haven't been home yet and these kids are getting on school buses.' It's not like we went out and celebrated, there were no celebrations, no wild drinking, we just sat and talked and ate. Finally, the exhaustion kicked in—you just didn't feel the exhaustion after something like that. Then, a couple of days later we went into Chicago, and we lost."

Have you ever had a bigger thrill in hockey than that goal?

"Well, yes—I would have to say winning the Stanley Cup that we won in Toronto in 1967. That was in my early years as a professional. The turning point in that year was when Punch Imlach got sick. We were on a losing streak, Imlach got sick, and King Clancy took over and we kinda put it together. They put Pulford, Pappin, and me together. I was the center guy who knocked people down, got the puck. Pappin had some speed down the wing, Pulford was a pretty tenacious guy, and we just clicked and everything worked out, and we ended up winning the Stanley Cup."

On his old boss, Emile Francis, and how no one ever seems to say a bad word about the guy:

"What can you say? I can sit here and say call me back in twenty-four hours, and I'll try to think of something, and I can't. He was just an honest hard worker, and he treated everybody the same—if you were the 50-goal scorer on the team or you were the guy on the fourth line and didn't dress, there were five, six rules, whatever, and you followed them. And I don't think anybody that ever was traded by Emile would have anything negative to say about him. I think those teams back then were his favorites; he comes back for alumni things. I was in Florida, called him up, said hello . . . I just feel he's very special. He's a very special person in hockey and a pretty special person in my life. I don't think I'm the only guy to say that. I have the highest respect for him.

"The only thing I feel bad about is we never won a Stanley Cup for him. It would have just been terrific. You just admired the guy. He practiced here in Long Beach, he jumped on the train, went into Madison Square Garden, probably got back seven, eight o'clock at night. He deserved the championship, and I really feel if there's one disappointment being with the Rangers it's that we never won one for the people in New York and for Emile Francis."

Does Francis get shortchanged historically because he didnt win a Cup?

"I think, what do you say, [something is missing] if a guy's involved twenty years in the major leagues and never wins a World Series or never wins a Super Bowl. It's always nice to win one. I think if Mario Lemiuex went through his entire career with all the numbers he put up and didn't win a Cup, I would think there would be a little bit of—maybe a little asterisk next to him. I don't think 'Cat' got shortchanged because of that, but I certainly don't think he didn't win because of lack of effort.

"Maybe he made some bad trades, but this is New York, and they're pretty demanding here. As far as I can see, I don't know how many bad trades he actually made, but he's respected. You never heard something that he said about you behind your back. If he didn't like the way you were playing or didn't like you, you knew right away. I mean, he'd call you in, and he'd look you in the eye, and I always respect anybody who's truthful and doesn't deny—like, 'I didn't say that.' He's a very highly respected guy

"I still get a chance to see his son, Bobby Francis, in Phoenix, and I always ask how Emile's doing, and his son is just very much like him. You can see, when I talk to Bobby, you know where he's coming from. He's got his father's input in him.

"No, I can't think of anything bad I could ever say about Emile Francis."

So, The Cat was different from other guys you dealt with?

"Well, I had Punch Imlach in Toronto, and everything with him was fear. He'd yell and scream at you. With Punch

Imlach back then, that was old school. Now, with Emile, if we got on the ice at 10:30 a.m., we knew at 11:30 a.m. we were coming off. With Punch Imlach, you got on at 10:30 a.m., you might be there until noon. If he didn't like the way you were practicing, he would just throw the pucks in the pail and say let's go do some skating. He was a real yeller-screamer, and Emile was more of an even-keel sort of guy. From Punch Imlach, what did I know? Then I went to Detroit and played for Sid Abel—I went from Toronto, which was Alcatraz, to Club Med, Sid Abel, we practiced twenty minutes. Alex Delvecchio, Gordie Howe, those guys were seasoned pros, and we didn't practice much there. Then we came to New York, where we worked hard, but it was just different."

On winning the faceoff that led to a Ron Harris overtime winner in Montreal in the 1974 playoffs:

"That faceoff win was against Pete Mahovlich. It was me against him, and I think that just as they went to drop the puck, Pete was distracted by something, whether he looked back to see whether the goalie [Bunny Larocque] was ready, or went to adjust his elbow pads. I just won the puck to Ronnie Harris, he just one-timed it, and it was over. It was one of those clean draws, right on his stick, in the net, and, hey, we went home. We were happy."

On the differences in the game now:

"Our trainer in New York was Frank Paice—a lovely guy, I think the world of Frank. Frank has passed on, but he wasn't an athletic trainer. He wasn't certified. I remember we used to have to take our own stitches out. A guy gets stitched up during a game, and they have to stay in five days or whatever, and Frank had a little bit of the shakes, so after five days, nobody wanted to go all the way to the doctor's office, sit there, and have him put the hydrogen peroxide on and get the scissors and cut them out. I remember Glen Sather used to take our stitches out for us. Trainer? Frank Paice was an usher between games. He'd go up in Madison Square Garden—he was an usher. Now, in any sport, you have to be certified. If something happens on the ice, you have to be able to jump out there and save a guy."

 **Rangers Trivia
#10**

Oh, good, another goalie question. During the 2000–01 season, the Rangers set a team record by using six goaltenders. One of them appeared in only one game, another in two, a third in four. You're a real Ranger fanatic if you can guess all six.

11

Fun and Games

You always have to be alert in a hockey locker room. Let your guard down, and you are likely to become a victim of a practical joke.

In the locker room, there would be twenty players and trainers and coaches. Anyone is capable of playing tricks on you, so you have to be ready.

Shaving cream in your skates, laces cut on your skates, and if you had false teeth, you had better make sure they weren't switched with somebody else's.

But any guy who pulled one of these pranks also had to know, in the back of his mind, that payback is a you-know-what. It's all part of being a team, and we were a team when I was with the Rangers. It was a great bunch of guys.

Creatures of Habit

Hockey players are very superstitious individuals, and our team showed it in the locker room.

First, there was the way some guys put on their hockey equipment before a game. Left skate on first, right skate on second. I myself had a routine—same routine every time I got dressed. I, too, would put my left skate on first, then my right—and I would do the same thing with my goalie pads.

After we dressed, Emile Francis would come in, shutting the locker room door. If the door was already closed, he would open it and shut it just to make sure everything was the same so he wouldn't disrupt anything. He was a creature of habit, too.

Now, the guys all knew of Emile's routine, so they would make sure to shut the door before he came in just to make him go through his little ritual. Everybody would laugh, including Emile.

The Cat would give us his little speech before going on the ice for the game, and we would leave the locker room in the same order—same order all the time. The goalies would go first and then the rest of the guys. It had to be the same every game. We didn't want to do anything to break our rhythm.

Shuffling the Deck

Peter Stemkowski remembers how much we used to all play cards together.

"Everybody today on the backs of planes plays cards, and we had our group that played cards. Sanderson used to play, Rolfe, Villemure, Brad Park—the card players. I remember very distinctly that we got stuck in Minneapolis with a big storm, and we were at the Thunderbird at the old stadium there, we had a half-day there. We didn't have a lot of time on the road then—the road trips weren't as big as they are now.

"Well, they played for half of a day, and I think Ron Greschner ended up just endorsing his paycheck and handing it to Villemure. And I know he used to take Greg Polis—he and Polis used to play cards all the time. I think it was gin rummy. Villemure used to tell me, 'I own that guy, I own that guy.' He loved playing with Greg Polis. I think he used to take Sanderson a little bit, too.

"Villemure liked the horses, and he liked to play cards, but it sure didn't bother his goaltending."

Slats and the Safe

Peter Stemkowski remembers a funny story about Glen Sather, one of our teammates and the guy running the show with the Rangers these days. He's the president now, having given up his GM duties.

"We used to leave our belongings in our pants pockets at Madison Square Garden. There was the Rangers locker room, then there was the medical room in the middle, and the other room was the Knicks' locker room. We used to just leave our wallets and our rings and watches in our pants pockets. I guess guys were starting to complain a little bit, whether it was the Knicks, or us, maybe there was a couple of bucks missing now and then.

"What they decided to do was put a wall safe in the medical room. Big enough to fit everybody's stuff, you could put your wallet and your ring and your watch in there during the game. Then, if somebody did get in, there would be nothing to steal in the room. So the first day we got it, the thing was open and only the trainer, Frank Paice, knew the combination. He was fiddling with it, closing it and opening it to make sure it worked all right.

"Well, Glen Sather walks in there, and said, 'So, this is the new wall safe, huh, Frank?' Frank said, 'Yeah,' He shut it, and within five minutes, Sather opened it. Somehow, he figured out the combination, opened it, and that was it for the safe.

"I don't know what that safe cost, but it was of no use anymore. He somehow figured it out.

"I guess right then and there we should have known that he was destined for bigger and better things."

New York's Finest

Bobby Orr once told my co-author a story about the night the Bruins won the Stanley Cup at Madison Square Garden.

After they beat us, the Bruins needed some help getting out of the Garden. Ranger fans in those days didn't like the Bruins and would let them know it—inside and outside the building. So, after they won, they were given a police escort through the streets of Manhattan on the way to the airport.

Orr said they got as far as the Midtown Tunnel, where the police were no longer needed. So, as the police cars peeled off to turn around and go back, the Bruins players waved thank-yous out the window and were greeted by one New York cop's salute—with one of his two middle fingers.

Hell hath no fury like a Rangers fan scorned.

The Streak

Rod Gilbert says nothing was offsides when it came to Peter Stemkowski.

"When I married my first wife in Florida, she had a shower," Rod recalls. "It was in 1974. Stemkowski and I were both getting married in June. About ten couples from the team had gone to Acapulco to the opening of the Acapulco Princess, and we all went there. We came back to Miami where my future wife was living, and she had about ten girlfriends over celebrating a shower. All the guys had dropped their wives and girlfriends, and we had two limousines, and we all went out to dinner ourselves.

"When we came back, Stemmer said to me, 'Hey, Rod, this has never been done before, in 1974, streaking is in the future groom's thing at your future wife's shower.' I said, 'Are you crazy? I don't even know three of the girls there. I can't do that.'

"Then he talked me into it. I said, 'Okay, if I do it, then will you do it with me?' He said, 'Fine.'

"So we come into the apartment, and I see all these gifts, you know, the Frederick's of Hollywood negligee. I picked that up, and I stuffed it into the back of my jeans, and I took him into the bedroom, and I said, 'Let's go.'

"He took all his clothes off, and I took all mine off. I put this negligee on with pompoms all over the place. I opened the door, and I pushed him out, and he was bare-assed. The girls were screaming, and I went real quick around the room, and I came back with my jeans and my shirt and it was a streak, right? Well, he didn't make it—he made it to the other side of the room, and he sat on the stereo there. He was like sitting down.

"Now, the girls were uncomfortable, and his future wife said to me, 'What's this all about?' I said, 'Gayle, it wasn't my idea.' So she said, 'Well, get him out of there.' I said, 'Stemmer, come on—you're not streaking now. Come on, you gotta end this.'

"He finally got up, looked at all the girls and said, 'What's the matter, girls? Didn't you ever see a 220-pound rocket with a one-inch fuse before?'

"That was funny, but that's the kind of humor he had. He was crazy. He could do a lot of stuff, but all in good fun. Nobody got hurt."

Another Streak

Eddie Giacomin relates the following story about Emile Francis getting the fellas out of trouble in, of all places, Colorado Springs:

"We had a week off and we went to Los Angeles," Eddie said. "We played a game, and we didn't fare too well, and he couldn't visualize us spending one whole week in Los Angeles. So he decided to take us to the Broadmoor Hotel in Colorado Springs. He had all the rules, that you can't drink in the building and all that. Of course, needless to say, we as a team broke every rule, and one of the players decided to streak down the hall.

"Well, this guy ran down the hall, and Walter Tkaczuk and I were at the end of the hall, and we reached out and pulled him in. The security people came, and they wanted to haul all three of us off to jail. Bill Jennings, the CEO of the Rangers then, was the one who had us go to the Broadmoor, and he got the gory details from Emile Francis and the people at the Broadmoor, but Emile stuck by us and said, 'You're taking me to jail before you take those guys to jail. He was a battler—small in stature but certainly big in heart, and they weren't taking his players anywhere.

"The next morning, at breakfast, you could hear the waiters saying, 'Did you hear about the Ranger player who was streaking down the hall last night?' It was hilarious."

Deli Day

Monday was usually our day off, and it was usually what we called our "Deli Day."

Said Eddie Giacomin: "If I got a shutout, in those days they used to pay you a hundred dollars, and if somebody got a hat trick, they'd get a hundred bucks. I would throw the hundred dollars into the pot, and we would go to practice at New Hyde Park. The majority of the time the coach wasn't there, so we would have Deli Day, and we would order beer and some sandwiches and whatever else. After practice, we'd go into the locker room and just BS. Sometimes, we'd have our children with us.

"The irony of it all, is that I can remember having 13 or 14 shutouts one year, and I was getting a hundred dollars, and [defenseman] Arnie Brown was getting two hundred bucks a shutout. At no time did we ever know that. Yet I was always throwing my hundred dollars in the pot, and he was always keeping his two hundred bucks in his pocket.

"We found out a long time down the road, and it was no big deal. But here I was willing to give up my hundred bucks for Deli Day, and somebody else was taking the bonus. I didn't expect him to give up his two hundred, but he could have contributed to the pot."

Spider-Man

Eddie Giacomin remembers one of his teammates turning into a cartoon character.

"We were at the Executive House in Chicago," Eddie says, "and we had a few drinks. We wanted to go down to the next floor to one of the other guy's rooms, and he wouldn't open the door. So, I think we were on the eleventh or twelfth floor and Fairbairn decided to play Spiderman. He just went over the balcony, down to the next balcony.

"If anything happened, he would have just splattered on the pavement down below. But, sure enough, there he was, and the guy had no choice but to open the door. He was out on the balcony. Needless to say, we got the door open, but thank goodness that Spiderman Fairbairn was the one that did it.

"This was in downtown Chicago. I'll never forget that as long as I live. We've told that story so many different times, it's unbelievable."

A Toothy Story

As you know, most hockey players lose some or all of their teeth. Eddie Giacomin is proud of the fact that he never lost any. Harry Howell never did, either. But teeth, especially missing ones, are an important part of any hockey team's lore.

"I happened to sit beside Walter Tkaczuk, and Fairbairn was there, and they were all getting ready," said Giacomin.

"I would see eight or nine or ten guys get ready for the game, and they always had their little plastic containers—they would take their teeth out and put them in the little plastic container, and I would watch these guys do it all the time. So I decided, 'I'm gonna change those teeth around.'

"So I would go through all those things and change everybody's teeth around. The game would be over, and we'd come back in and the guys would put their teeth in and say 'Eddie, you son of a B.' And, of course, the next day in practice, where are they going to shoot the puck? All at my head, hoping to hit me in the teeth.

"This went on constantly. But at no time, though, in my 10 years in New York, did anyone ever hit my face. They came close a couple of times, they tried hard, but I had so much fun mixing those teeth up."

Wanting to Be Me

I can't imagine why anyone else besides me would want to be me, but that's exactly what happened to me when I was playing for the New York Rangers.

There was a guy driving around the New York area in a van that had the words "Paul Villemure, New York Rangers Scouting Department" written on the side. He claimed to be my brother, but was also passing himself off as me. Apparently, he was trying to convince young hockey players to tour colleges with him, and there was a feeling he was doing it for sexual reasons.

Frank Torpey, the head of security for the National Hockey League, was made aware of what was going on and set up a sting that saw him accompany a kid to a meeting. Torpey was accompanied by a couple of FBI friends, and they did a good job of scaring the imposter, whose real name was Paul Kostofsky.

They peeled the words, which were actually stuck on, off the van, and sent him on his way with a strong warning and a good scare. But this wasn't over.

Kostofsky was using my name to get dates. Now, Rod Gilbert was known as the lady-killer on our team, but this guy was saying he was Gilles Villemure, and I think he even had a helicopter that he used to pick up women. He went all the way with this thing.

Did it work? Well, I was doing a card show in New Jersey, and a girl approached me at the table. She said, "You're not Gilles Villemure—I'm going out with Gilles Villemure, and you're not Gilles Villemure. I'm going out with him, and I should know."

I said, "Lady, here's my driver's license," and showed it to her. She almost fell on the floor. She kept looking at me and saying, "You're not Gilles Villemure." Isn't that something?

I guess this was going on for a long time, because the card show was after I finished playing. I guess he had money to be able to pull something like this off. He used to fly in to meet girls on this helicopter.

As Rodney Dangerfield used to say, "It ain't easy being me." Little did I know it took the work of two of us to get the job done.

12

A Little Help from My Friends
Vic Hadfield

"It always seemed to me that Gilles was just a special guy. By that I mean he was so dedicated, he really wanted to help the hockey club in any area that he possibly could. We could see that he had a tremendous amount of skill and determination. He wanted to win. He was very much a team type of a player who would do anything. He didn't have an opportunity to play a lot because Ed Giacomin was our main goalie, but we as players felt very comfortable when Emile did make a change and put Gilly in. It didn't really matter to us because we had so much confidence in Gilly's ability.

Vic Hadfield became the first Ranger to score 50 goals, in 1971–72.
(New York Rangers)

"He was a fiery kind of guy, great off the ice, great with his teammates, and I think he's just turned out to be one of the nicest fellas that I've had the opportunity to meet.

"He did get started late but didn't give up. Back then there were only six teams with six goalies, and there was a tremendous amount of other players in the same position as Gilly. Denis Dejordy came to mind—he played in the minors for a lot of years before he went up, and with Gilly it just showed what type of individual he was. We had a pretty strong goaltending duo there with Eddie and Gilly.

They won the Vezina Trophy that first year together, and when we started out the first of the year, we tried to keep our goals down to less than two a game. A lot of years we were able to do that with the type of team that we had and strong goalkeeping. Gilly was right up there and equal to Eddie Giacomin.

"They both came from the same mold. Gilly had a little different temperment than Eddie. Eddie was the one who played most of the games, but Gilly was preparing himself for whenever he was needed.

"Gilly was a great guy back then, and he's still the same type of guy today. He helps me in some of the golf tournaments I run in New York for different foundations. He's always readily available with a big smile on his face, and the people just love him."

On Emile Francis:

"No one ever worked harder than Emile. I used to call back in July to New York and say, 'How's everything?' He would have just had his lunch—he brought his lunch from home because he didn't want to leave the office. He wasn't out in all the restaurants around New York City. He stayed right in the office, and, being a player and hearing those types of things, you see just how dedicated he was to having a winning team. And that rubbed off down to the players—the guys would go through brick walls for him. It was just unfortunate that we weren't able to win the Stanley Cup back then, but we certainly tried, and Emile couldn't have been a better coach or general manager in New York. It's a difficult city, as most people know, and he certainly gave it his 100 percent."

On the Rangers perhaps being the best team ever that didn't win a Stanley Cup:

"It was unfortunate that Jean Ratelle broke his ankle, and we just didn't have anybody to replace him, which would have been difficult on any team because he meant so much to us. I would have to say that that was probably one of the better teams that didn't win."

On whether there was a feeling that year that the 1971–72 team was special right from the start:

"All the teams went to training camp with the thought that, 'Geez, you know, we have a pretty good squad here, and our main objective is to win the Stanley Cup.' Personal goals meant nothing to any of the players back then, whether you scored 30 goals, 50 goals, or 10 goals. We dedicated ourselves to winning that Stanley Cup. We were always reminded that New York hadn't won in so many years, and you look around the room, and you see the squad that we had there, with All-Star defensemen and centermen and two top goalkeepers and with a little luck we could be there. We came awful close, but it just wasn't good enough. You have to be very lucky and not have the injuries, and we were just unfortunate to lose a player of Jean Ratelle's capabilities. He meant so much to us, and we just couldn't recover."

On his fondest moment:

"I don't want to sound corny, but coming from Canada, I wanted to be a hockey player. In my little hometown there of Oakville, Ontario, there were about fifteen or twenty guys that had shown some ability when they were fourteen, fifteen years of age. That's all I wanted to do—play hockey. I neglected school because I wanted to grab as much ice time as I possibly could, and I was one of the very fortunate ones to come out of Oakville and have a chance to play pro hockey. So when you're asking me what would be the most important thing, I'd have to say it was putting on that New York Ranger sweater back in 1960.

"On the ice, with that team, there's a few things. I mean, your ultimate goal is to win the Stanley Cup. Personal things don't mean anything if you don't win. That's how everybody felt. I know I was very fortunate to have the opportunity to play with guys like Gilly and Eddie Giacomin, Brad Park, Emile Francis, playing on a line with Jean Ratelle and Rod Gilbert. That was a big thing. And I was lucky enough to score 50 goals in 1972. That was also a highlight, but they were all secondary as far as I'm concerned, and I don't dwell on it even today because we didn't win. If we had won and I had scored 50 goals, that would have been great, but we didn't win, and so you feel like you cheated, and you didn't give enough, but we certainly tried, and it just wasn't meant to be."

On the Rangers being a very close group:

"Oh, very tight. Very tight—you don't see that today. There was a tremendous bond. We have our alumni golf tournaments, and you might not have seen an individual for ten years, but as soon as you sit down, it's like you were with him yesterday. We always traveled together in New York. Bruce MacGregor and Glen Sather and I drove to practices and to the games. The three wives would drive in together, and then the six of us would go out and have dinner afterwards. It wasn't just us six—half of the team would be at an Italian place, and the rest of the team would maybe want Chinese, so we were always together after games and as families. We were very, very tight."

On whom he has stayed in closest contact with over the years:

"I'm in touch with Rod Gilbert a lot in New York, and Gilles Villemure. Bobby Nevin's here, Andy Bathgate, and Harry Howell. We have a pretty good group right here in the Toronto area. Rod Seiling's here, working for the hotel association."

13

Life Away from the Ice

Harness Racing

Besides playing hockey I was a harness racing driver, trainer, and owner—something, like hockey, that is in my past, even though I still enjoy going to the track.

I started to drive horses when I was seventeen years old. The hockey rink and the racetrack were side by side in my hometown. After the hockey season was over, I would go back to my hometown and drive horses. It used to keep me in shape. In 1970, I won the driving title.

I could have easily made a career for myself in harness racing, but I chose to play hockey full-time and make harness racing a part-time thing.

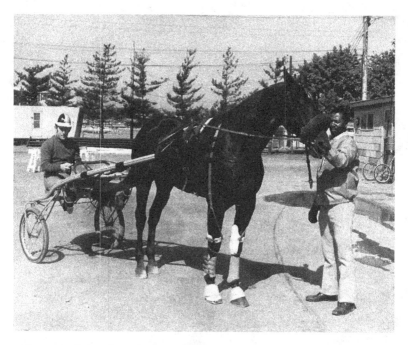

This is me behind my first New York horse, Guy Bristol. My son Bobby's and daughter Denise's favorite. They played with him all the time. (Gilles Villemure)

No one in hockey ever bothered me about driving horses during my off season, not even Emile Francis. When we reported to training camp, he would always ask me how I did driving over the summer, and if I had won many races.

For me, it was the perfect setup—hockey in the winter and harness racing in the summer. I was involved in sports all year round.

I raced at many of the major racetracks—Montreal, Quebec, Trois Rivieres (my hometown), Roosevelt (which is now gone), Monticello, Freehold, and The Meadowlands. I had a lot of fun driving horses.

I got out in 1990. The game was changing. I had only one horse left, and it was very expensive to buy horses. So I just decided that's enough, and I stopped.

When people ask me if harness racing is fixed, my answer is simple—"fix" is a big word. "Fix" is a very, very big word. You can get help in the race, but I don't think you should call that fixed. You have eight drivers; you might get help, but I don't think that's fixed. There were some fixed races, but the guys got caught, and they don't have a license anymore. They're out.

When I was driving, I wasn't aware of anything. But I knew one thing—in the race, the guys pop on the outside of you, and there's two things you can do. You let him go or you park him. If you want to help yourself win the race, if it's better to let him go, you let him go. If it's better to park him, you park him. And people say, "Oh, he let him go, he let him go," and they say it's fixed. It doesn't go that way.

It's an athletic competition. You have to do the best you can, and every race is different. There were some fixed races, of course, but the guys got caught and got thrown out, and they're still not racing.

I still go to the track. I go out to Belmont to watch thoroughbreds almost every Saturday. I go to the Meadowlands three or four times a year. They closed Roosevelt down. Yonkers is up, and I think it will come back big time with the slot machines. They did it in Ontario and the game is big. They did it with Dover Downs; the purses are great, people are working—and I know New York State will do the same. They need those slot machines. The slots make the difference.

Near Return

After I left the Rangers, I played only 21 more games in the National Hockey League with Chicago over two seasons. We didn't make the playoffs. But as it turned out, John Ferguson almost brought me back to New York after he took over as head of the Rangers. Almost.

I can't remember who got hurt for the Rangers, but Fergie had me traded back to New York. Our third goaltender in Chicago got hurt, and they couldn't trade me anymore. As a matter of fact, I was back on Long Island for a week; we had a week off and I was hurt or something, and I heard Fergie said I was traded back to New York.

I was coming back, and I would have been happy to come back. I settled in New York after my playing career ended, so it would have been great to finish my career here. The Rangers were struggling at the time, but it still would have been nice to end my career where it all started, with the people I knew.

Why I Stayed

Even though I'm a French-Canadian, I decided to stay in the New York area after my playing days were over, and it's been home ever since.

I married an American girl. I've been married twice. My first wife came from East Northport, Long Island, which is why I stayed here. Then, my second wife came from Levittown. When I got divorced, my kids were young, and I could have gone to Edmonton. Glen Sather was in the World Hockey Association at the time, and he called me and said,

"Gilly, I have a job for you. If you want to come out with us [as a player] for a year or two, you have a job." I said, "Glen, I can't do it. I have two young kids here, and I can't move away." I retired, but that's why I stayed here. It was because of my kids.

My kids and their ages: Denise, 50, Bobby, 49, Therese, 37, Natalie, 32 (she's the baby).

Hall of Fame

One of the greatest things that ever happened to me just took place in January 2002. I was inducted into the Trois Rivieres Sports Hall of Fame. There was a special ceremony, my wife, my kids, and I went home, and about 700 people were there. All my friends were there, my family was there, my mom, my brothers. It was great thrill for me.

There are other names you might remember in that Hall of Fame. Andre "Moose" Dupont was selected. I was in the Ranger organization with Moose before he went on to bigger and better things in Philadelphia. Rene Robert, one-third of Buffalo's French Connection line, is another name in there. Leon Rochefort, another ex-Ranger, who also played for a half-dozen other teams, is in there.

It was a very nice thing.

Rangers Alumni

Steve Vickers, Bill Chadwick, and John Halligan are the three guys who started the Ranger Alumni Association. Now the Rangers have taken it over.

It was started to help former players in trouble. We had a golf outing, we had old-timer's games. Management of the organization would change every two or three years; it got put on the backseat for awhile, when nobody took care of it. Now we have a corporation, and we have people working for the alumni now.

I do things connected with the organization, but I wish I could do more. We have golf outings once a year, a couple of games. We have the legends box at the Garden, and every game they sell this box to twenty or thirty people, and I go sit with the fans, sign autographs. I wish I could do more. I'm retired—just call me and I'll do it. I don't mind going places to represent the Rangers.

The alumni events help me keep track of where the guys are now, and it's not easy.

As I've said, this was a very close group, on and off the ice. I could talk about twenty guys, all great guys. We used to have parties—Rod Seiling used to invite us all over to his house. We were a great bunch of guys who stuck together. Time and distance have separated us, but we still love getting together whenever we can, for whatever function.

It's always great to see the guys whenever I can. Lots of fun. Lots of old stories. Once a teammate, always a teammate.

They Never Forget

One thing about New York Rangers fans—once you're in their hearts, they don't forget you. People still remember me around New York. I go on the train to go into the Garden, and people say, "Hey, Villemure?" They're looking at me, they know me.

I go to restuarants or bars sometimes with my wife and they remember. They remember who we were.

It was a special time for hockey. It was a special time for the New York Rangers, and those people don't forget. A lot of them were right there when the Rangers finally won the Stanley Cup in 1994, and that's a special thing about hockey in New York.

14

A Little Help from My Friends
Rod Seiling

"Gilles, through no fault of his own, took a long time to get to the National Hockey League. He was always a very good goaltender and certainly showed that during the years he was with the Rangers. He was much different than Eddie in style and temperment, and they complemented each other. Eddie got much more publicity, but I've always felt that Gilles was his equal. They both contributed to our overall success.

"Giles's personality was much more easygoing, kind of laid-back, took things in stride, great temperment for a goaltender, was a great team player."

Rod Seiling and I spent a great deal of time together—both on the ice and at the racetrack. (New York Rangers)

On Villemure's love of horses and harness racing:

"I must have spent more time with Gilles than anybody on the team. We spent a lot of time at the racetrack. I'm out of it now—I retired to work in the horse racing industry. I had my own farm and owned horses but also ran a racetrack and did some things, and when I moved on, I was with the Ontario Jockey Club, which was the largest operator in North America. I wasn't allowed to own horses when I worked there, so I had to sell my horses, and I've just never gotten back into it. I bought my first horse (Gilles and I knew a guy at Roosevelt Raceway) and shipped it up here.

"We used to kid Gilly. Gilly was always buying horses, and we'd say, 'You sure you know how many horses you've got, and where are they and what are they doing?' Before we went to practice every morning, he and I would go to Roosevelt and jog and train horses. We had a great time—it was a great outlet from the wars of hockey. We really enjoyed it, and we got to know some people there. Gilles was responsible for my involvement with horses—if it wasn't for him, I wouldn't have gotten involved to the degree I did."

Is this the best team that never won a Stanley Cup?

"I would think so, but who knows—there are others that may disagree. But 'should have, could have'—all those markers apply to us, I guess. They're reasons, excuses, and at the end of the day, I guess that's all they were—excuses, because the simple fact is we *didn't win*. We were certainly good enough to win and should have won but did not win, and at the end of the day, I guess that's all that counts.

"There are players who never get as close as we did, but that still doesn't take it away. I think if you talk to the players on that team, the vast majority of them never did end up winning a Stanley Cup. If there's one missing element of their career, that would be it. It certainly is mine. I mean, I'm not lying awake at night crying over it, but certainly we all would love to have been able to say we were Stanley Cup winners, and we can't. To say we could is just it—the hockey gods were not kind to us."

Was there a feeling among guys on the team at the time that something would always happen in March to mess up April and May?

"I don't think so. You put that out of your mind. You think if we're good enough to win, we'll win, and you do your best, and, unfortunately, something came up during all those things that took away from the ultimate victory. The Ratelle injury and other factors certainly hurt, but you can also say good players play through those things."

On his feelings about Emile Francis:

"The Cat demanded—with reason—respect and was a very good hockey man, a tough taskmaster, but fair. He expected his players to be as competitive and as dedicated as he was. He never let up, and we went as hard the last day of training camp as we did the first day. That's the way he went at it. No one put more in the team on a personal commitment than he did. On the other hand, he expected his players to be the same.

"I've never seen a dressing room yet where the coach and general manager are universally loved, that's the nature of the beast. But, on the other hand, to give him his due, I think he was respected by all. Some may not have agreed with everything he did—I don't see how you can run a team and have every person on that team agree with everything you did. That's an impossibility. But I think it's equally truthful to say he was respected by everybody within that room."

On what it meant to him when the Rangers finally won the Stanley Cup in 1994:

"From my perspective, being an ex-Ranger, people stopped asking: 'When are the Rangers ever going to win a Stanley Cup?' From that perspective alone—I was pleased for the players that were there, don't get me wrong. But from a personal perspective, those questions stopped immediately. There's never been a question since, which is *nice*.

"I was watching [Game 7 against Vancouver] at home. I had the opportunity to go to New York to watch the game, and I just couldn't get away. It turned out to be quite a wise decision because they did pan down and show a whole bunch of ex-Rangers at the game. They had them stuck in their own corner there, and I would have had to dodge out of an important business meeting, and it would not have been a wise career move to have my picture flashed at the game at Madison Square Garden when I was supposed to be back here in Toronto at a meeting."

On his life as one of the Garden fans' whipping boys during his stay in New York:

"They weren't [nice to me]. I respect fans and their right to have opinions. I think it goes within reason, and I thought toward the end of my career in New York they far outstripped that, and that's why I reacted back. I knew The Cat wasn't in a position to do anything—his own position was tenuous at best, and I just took matters into my own hands. I just made a few comments about the fans.

"It got nasty and very personal, and it got personal for my wife and kids and that's where I drew the line and said, 'Enough is enough.' I didn't think they had any right—do what you want, say what you want about me, but when you go at my family, that's where I draw the line.

"They were looking for someone to be a goon, and that wasn't me, nor would it ever have been me."

On missing New York in spite of the way the fans treated him:

"I still have friends there. I go back to New York on a regular basis. I think it's a great city. I love New York. I almost came back and worked there ten or twelve years ago. But for reasons, nothing to do with New York, I'd be back there now. I actually accepted a job and then some other things came up. I love the city, I like what it has to offer and was just back two months ago with very good friends, other ex-players, for a surprise birthday party. I had a great time."

On his proudest achievement in hockey:

"I think the 1972 [Summit Series] team—Team Canada beating the Russians would be right up there. It's still marked as the greatest event in hockey, at least in [Canada], and I suspect anywhere. I just came back from Russia, and it's still the major topic over there."

15

A View of the Game

Editor's Note: This chapter was written for the book's original publication in 2002.

Best of the Blue

With the New York Rangers having passed the 75th anniversary of the start of the great franchise, I have seen some all-time Rangers teams pop up. Two lists came out at the turn of the new century, and we'll throw two more in here for you.

One list was by John Davidson, who came to New York to take over the goaltending from me and Eddie Giacomin and carried the Rangers to the Stanley Cup finals in 1979—another near miss.

Writing in John Halligan's great book, *New York Rangers: Seventy-Five Years,* J. D., who is now the president of hockey operations for the Columbus Blue Jackets, picked Mike

The game may be quicker today, but goaltenders had to make more saves back when I played. (Gilles Villemure)

Richter as the all-time Rangers goaltender, with Brad Park and Brian Leetch on defense, Mark Messier at center, Rod Gilbert on the right wing, and Adam Graves on the left.

The other list I saw in print appeared on NYRangers.com, as voted by the fans. There was only one difference from the Davidson picks—Vic Hadfield, the first Ranger to score 50 goals, was the left wing, instead of Graves, who also had a 50-goal season, has his number retired, and now works for the Rangers.

Emile Francis, our great coach when I played with the Rangers, picks Chuck Rayner as the goaltender, Park and Leetch on defense (over Tim Horton, who wasn't with us that long but made quite an impression on The Cat while he was), and the G-A-G Line up front, all three of them.

Rayner? "I saw Rayner the year that the Rangers could have won the Stanley Cup [1950], and he carried them on his back," The Cat says. "He played there with hardly any support at all, as did Gump Worsley for a number of years."

My picks? Remember, I don't have the background going way back with the franchise. But I'll take a shot. And I'm only picking retired players.

How can I not go with Eddie Giacomin in goal? It wouldn't make sense. I had the pleasure of playing with that man for five years, and I know what he did to help put the Rangers at the top of the National Hockey League. True, Richter was able to win a Stanley Cup, and he even stopped Pavel Bure with that unbelievable penalty shot save, but Eddie's my choice as No. 1 overall.

On defense, my choices would be Brad Park and Harry Howell, but Brian Leetch had a great career and his number is also retired.

Up front, I have to go with the G-A-G Line—Rod Gilbert, Jean Ratelle, and Vic Hadfield, with Gilbert in a close nod over Andy Bathgate, one of the greatest Rangers of all time.

The Best I've Seen

We've talked about my all-time Rangers team. Now, it's on to the best I've seen overall.

In goal, I'd have to go with Kenny Dryden, Eddie Giacomin, Tony Esposito, Bernie Parent, and Gerry Cheevers. In no particular order. It would be very, very tough to pick one guy out of that list.

Oh, by the way, they're all in the Hall of Fame.

Defense? Well, Bobby Orr. That's an easy one. Then I'd go with Brad Park and Denis Potvin, the great Islanders defensemen.

Yes, these three are in the Hall of Fame, too.

On left wing, I'd have to go with Bobby Hull, the man with the incredible shot. Behind him, I'd have to name Frank Mahovlich.

Two Hall of Famers.

On right wing, Yvan Cournoyer was great. So was Rod Gilbert.

Two more Hall of Famers. I guess I have an eye for the better players.

Bigger Bodies . . . But

People are always telling me how the game has changed since I was playing. Remember, I left the National Hockey League almost forty years ago, so you know a lot of things have to be different. Heck, sometimes I have to read the standings in the paper every morning just to catch up on how many teams there are now. The league has grown 500 percent since I came in, and the players have grown, too.

The kids are more physical; they're bigger, stronger. You have to give them credit—they are. We didn't have all the stuff they have—the weight room, bicycles. We didn't have anything. And we had to work at other jobs during the off season. Now, they can work out, and they have their own personal trainers to help them stay in shape. These kids are in terrific shape these days. They work at it.

But I think the skill level in our day was better. Maybe people will disagree with me. But we had guys like Jean Ratelle, Stan Mikita, Guy LaFleur, all those guys, making plays. These days, very seldom do they make plays in the center. They shoot the puck in and go get it, play dump and chase. In our day, players carried the puck and made plays—we never shot the puck in. We just carried it in. That was a big difference, but now, because the kids are so big, they can't carry it in anymore. They take up the whole ice, some of these guys playing today.

We used to make more plays. We had more shots on goal. Many games were 40–45 shots. Now, if you see 25 shots a game, 30? . . . that's a lot. There was more action back then, more shots—I mean, Phil Esposito had 15 shots on goal against me in one game. But I've seen some games in the last couple of years with the Rangers, in which there were 18, 15, 12 shots on goal. We handled the puck more, we took more chances, and maybe had more room to move, which led to chances.

As the generation of new buildings grew in the NHL, they had the chance to make the surfaces bigger, which would have allowed the game itself to grow at the same rate as its players. The door was open, and they didn't walk in. Now, you've got these huge men playing this game on the same surface we played on, and there's just no room. This is a much bigger game now.

The game was better to watch then—the goaltenders had to make more saves. But now, it's quick—my God it's quick! Especially in the playoffs—you have no chance to do anything. You have to get rid of the puck because if you don't, you'll get in trouble. It's dangerous now, the kids are so strong—and there's not enough room on the ice.

Better? I was playing then, in the seventies, so I would ask the fans what was better to watch. It's hard for me to tell because I played the game. But more shots, more saves, more goals, more chances—I think that's the name of the game.

The game has changed in the way players settle things, too. Years ago, they used to drop the gloves. They have visors on their helmets now and that's changed everything. When I played, you fight, you fight for five minutes, ten minutes, you're so tired you can't lift your arms up, you can't do anything. Some guys got hurt—cut, not hurt—but not usually

There was one time that Bobby Hull had a broken jaw, and John Ferguson, one of the toughest there ever was, ripped the football helmet Hull was wearing off and broke the jaw again. But there was one time John Ferguson was good to Hull. Bobby was on the ice, and Fergie was on top of him and really could have pounded him. And he said, "Get up." He could have killed him, but Fergie backed out.

16

A Little Help from My Friends
Bill Fairbairn

"Did anyone tell you about the thing that happened in Oakland?

"We flew into Oakland, and we had a practice. We had won a game, and we were going to have a practice in the morning, around ten o'clock, and we all got to the rink, and Stemmer's idea came: 'Let's get The Cat.' So, they filled his whistle up with shaving cream so it wasn't working, and then Stemmer got his gloves and filled them up; Dale Rolfe found a hammer and beat the crap out of his blades so it was hard for him to stand up, and then on the way out, we all headed out to the ice, and Stemmer put Vaseline all over the door handle so he couldn't really turn that.

"What Stemmer had done really made The Cat mad. He was in a bad mood in the first place, and he comes out on the ice, and he's madder than heck at what we had done, and he's going to really skate us, eh? But the thing was that Stemmer had talked to the rink guy to tell him after about ten minutes to shut off all the lights. Well, Cat started skating us, and all the lights went off, and we had to leave the rink and there was no practice.

"We had a blast there. That was just part of a team—we knew what was going to happen. The Cat was mad, and he started skating us, and we knew the lights were going out.

"[Cat] just kinda giggled and that was it. He says, 'Okay, you guys have had your fun—until the next practice.' That's the way he was."

On being part of such a close group:

"I wouldn't give up the years I played in New York with that team for anything. It was like one big family. We stuck together, not just on game days. When we had days off, we all got together, the wives got together, and everybody enjoyed each other. After practices we even hung around together. It's something that doesn't happen now in the game. I think it's more of a business than it was back then. I can really appreciate it because I have a lot of friends from back then. I don't get to see them that often but when we do it's just like we've never been apart. I don't know what I can say about that team, but it was a great team."

On the craziest guy he ever played with:

"Oh, I would think Stemmer. He was a case, that guy. He was a fun person that kept everybody laughing, all the time."

On The Cat:

"He worked so hard at it, and hard at it, and hard at it, and he had all the respect of all the players. He wasn't very big, but I'll tell ya, most of the guys were scared of him—I would say all of them—and really did want to win for him. I couldn't have had a better coach in hockey, ever. He got you going. He did a lot to get the team built up and everything else. He would do anything for the team and expected it back. Everybody respected him and would do anything for him."

On the Rangers goaltending duo:

"I thought we had two of the best in the league. I think they competed against each other, even in practice, to see who would be the game goalie. They really had to work hard in practice, too. They were both exceptional goalies, and you don't usually get that on a team. Usually you have one that is quite a bit better than the other. We were lucky there to have two really exceptional goalies, even one who would come up big in a game. It was great for the team."

On Canadians living in New York:

"It was different. I have to admit that. Coming from a small town, like I did—Brandon, Manitoba—and going right into New York was kind of a shock. I think the big thing that really relaxed me and a lot of the players was the fans. The fans we had there were just great. They were just part of the team, too, and it kind of relaxed you on the ice. Outside the building, it was a different situation altogether, a little scary in the big city, but as soon as you got into the Garden and all the fans were there . . . and we had good players and had winning teams there, and it made a difference. The fans and their backing just helped everybody fit in and work together. I couldn't have gone to a better city to play hockey."

Do you remember your first day in Manhattan?

"I don't remember the first one, but I remember back when Martin Luther King was shot. I was staying in a hotel and went outside. I think there were ten policemen at every corner of the streets down there, and I was just going for a walk. I turned around and stayed in my hotel the rest of the day. It was a scary moment, and I think that was the first time I was brought up from Omaha to play. It was a scary time.

"As I said, though, once I got into the Garden, the fans kinda took care of you—they took you under their wing. They looked after you. You played well for them, they appreciated it. If you gave a 100 percent effort, they liked that. New York fans don't like to lose, I know that, but in those days when I first came up, we were winning, and we didn't lose too many at home that year, so that helped out a lot. It took a lot of the pressure off and made you feel more at home; just being in the Garden was a different matter than being outside."

On taking a hit to make a play:

"Even from my junior days, I was more or less kind of a hitter and a grinder. Nothing really bothered me. I felt more comfortable along the boards than the way the game's played now, with crisscrossing and everything else. And playing with Walter [Tkaczuk] was a big factor, too. We kinda read each other, and that helped a lot. He would give me the puck, and if I had to take a hit, he would be there to pick up the puck and vice-versa. Playing with a solid guy like him was a great help, too."

On the great Tkaczuk-Fairbairn penalty-killing duo:

"When we first came up, The Cat came to us and just said we would be doing most of the penalty killing, and he wanted us because we were young, had a lot of speed, and could take the bumps and grinds and it wouldn't wear us down. That was one of the main reasons, I think, he had us killing penalties."

On the Rangers finally winning the Cup in 1994:

"Once a Ranger, always a Ranger. Anybody that was ever on the Ranger team, even if they played for other teams before that . . . I don't know, I think it's because of the city and everything else and the fans and everything. Just being part of a winning team is just great. Maybe we never did win the Cup while I was playing, but to be part of the Rangers when they won, it is an honor."

On his fondest memory of his Rangers days:

"There are so many of them, but I guess going to the Stanley Cup against Boston. I guess that was the biggest feat and most important in my hockey career. Losing was a big disappointment, a real big disappointment. Every time I watch TV now, I just wonder if maybe there was a little more I could have done to get that Cup. But you can't, and it's hard when you see the Stanley Cup on there, and they show different teams winning and pointing to the Cup, and your name isn't there. It's pretty disheartening when you know you could have won that year.

"We had a few years there, even when the Islanders beat us out in overtime. We could have had a chance that year and the other year when Philly won it, and we had a chance, we were there. We were right there, three years in a row we could have won, but we didn't."

17

A New Beginning

Sometimes, a guy you've played against and hated, in a hockey sense, anyway, winds up becoming your teammate. Sometimes, guys identified with one team suddenly wind up playing for that team's biggest rival. Derek Sanderson, Phil Esposito, and Carol Vadnais all became Rangers; Jean Ratelle and Brad Park moved to the Bruins. It's the nature of the business.

On June 6, 2002, the Rangers named Bryan Trottier as their new head coach, replacing Ron Low. Bryan Trottier, Mr. Islander!

"He was a hard-working player. I would imagine that's the reason they got him," my old teammate, Billy Fairbairn, said of the new coach. "I had a lot of respect for Trottier, a lot of respect in those years. He wasn't a chippy, or a cheap hockey player. He was a hard-working hockey player. It would be a little different if it was somebody that didn't earn it, but he did, I think.

"He deserves it. He's a proven part of hockey as a player and a coach. I just hope he can swing the team the right way We need to get into the playoffs."

No. 99, Wayne Gretzky, told the *New York Post,* "I think the Rangers made a great choice. I think they have a great coach . . . he's very sharp. I'm sure he's going to succeed there."

Well, it didn't quite work out.

18

A Little Help from My Friends
Ted Irvine

Teddy Irvine took the shot that Peter Stemkowski converted into the winning goal in the third overtime period of that incredible game against Chicago in 1971.

"When you get in situations like that, you wonder where you get the adrenaline from to hang on. You just do. The conditioning pays off. I remember it more because I remember the picture more than anything else. The puck thrown into the corner—and what I remember was the explosion. I threw it out front, and Stemmer had deflected the puck in, and I think the explosion from the fans with that goal going in and then the reaction of the guys all jumping together—I think it was a relief that we were finally off the ice after a long game.

"The fans' explosion and roar—things like that happen so fast. It's a shot in the corner, it's out front and it's in the net, just like that, and you think, 'Why didn't you do that earlier?' That's what I remember more than anything else."

On how good that team really was:

"It was an outstanding team. To this day, people still talk about that team. I found, being on the line I was on, with Stemmer and MacGregor, and then Jerry Butler . . . we all had a role on that hockey club, whether it be Bard Park, to Gilles Villemure, to Eddie Giacomin, to Stemkowski or Irvine. That's what I found to be the biggest strength of that hockey club—we all respected each other and the role we had to play and what type of game that individual had to play well and do his job.

"There's no greater thrill in my life than being able to sit here and, say, Jean Ratelle would come to me and say, 'What a great goal you got, Teddy,' when he's one of the great goal scorers ever, or somebody would come to you and say, 'nice fight,' or 'way to backcheck,' and then you'd be going to those superstars and saying, 'Brad, nice play,' and 'Rod Seiling, nice defensive play.' I found it an unselfish bunch of guys. We all had a role to play, Emile Francis played us equally, and there was a lot of pride on that team, as far as respect for each other."

On wanting to win the Cup for Emile Francis:

"To this day as I sit and talk to my own family of all the things we don't have, there's that Stanley Cup ring. And when you get thirty years out of the game, you look back and say,

'What was it all about—yeah, it was fun and it was great playing in New York and it was fun playing in front of the fans.' But you can't look at that finger and say you have that Stanley Cup ring. And Emile Francis was such a gentleman and a true . . . he was almost like a father to me. I remember that when I got traded from Los Angeles, he lent me money for my first house, and we look back now, all the things he did for us personally, how he protected us and how he stood up for us and how he scolded us and how he skated the heck out of us and taught us lessons. If you look back, there was such a relationship there with Emile, I think every one of the players would say the same thing. It would be nice to have a Stanley Cup ring, but, just ego-wise, it would be nice for Emile Francis to go into Boston and Montreal and say, 'Hey, I got one, too.' I think that hurts him more than anything, not having the ring. And us not giving Emile his day. I remember we played in Chicago against Billy Reay, and we had a team meeting before and Emile said, 'You guys go out and you'll fight your hearts out, and I'll stand up for you,' and during the game he was yelling at Billy Reay and he was going to fight Billy Reay. We just looked at him and said, 'Hey, this guy's on our side,' and not getting him the ring is just as important and sad as us not getting one either."

On what the players did to The Cat, as jokes:

"I remember a lot of things the boys did to Emile, and that's why I say what a man he was. We knew how far we could go with him as a coach and as a man. He let us go so far, but then there were other days, too, where you just stayed out of his way. When Emile wasn't happy with us . . . we'd get off the plane, you talk about discipline, if we'd played a bad game, he'd get the ice somewhere, and we'd have to go from the airport right to the rink and he would skate the heck out of us. In Oakland, they turned the lights off, and Emile said, 'I don't care, these guys are still skating.'

"I remember a time we lost in Los Angeles, and they took us into Toronto. We got off the plane at four or five o'clock, and he skated the heck out of us for two hours and just wouldn't stop. No pucks, and he skated us and skated us and we were just dragging ourselves. I remember Walter Tkaczuk yelling, 'One more time, Cat,' and away we'd go again. We're saying, 'Walter, SHUT UP!' But Emile, he skated us and skated us, but also there were times when he knew to let up a little bit, too.

"We used to do things to him. I remember what Vic Hadfield did to him. Emile had a habit of coming into the dressing room and picking up a piece of tape and throwing it in the garbage. That was kind of a routine he had. We were winning a little bit, so Vic just tied a string on to the tape and Emile bent over to pick it up and he just pulled it away from him. We had a great laugh and Emile was a good enough sport to laugh, too. But when we lost, he didn't think it was funny—he came after us pretty good."

On his rather famous son, wrestler Chris Jericho:

"Chris Jericho, Y2J, was born in Jericho, New York, a Ranger fan, still a huge Ranger fan, has an opportunity to play in Madison Square Garden in the Christopher Reeve Foundation game. He just absolutely loves his hockey, so he's played at the NHL All-Star Game and he's played at Madison Square Garden. This past year I had the chance to play against him, and he and I had a full-scale brawl at center ice, and I'm proud to say I gave it to my son."

How did the wrestling thing get started with Chris?:

"When we came back to Winnipeg when Chris was fifteen or sixteen, he started lifting weights. He just said, 'Dad, I want to give it a try.' So we took him up to Calgary, and he went to wrestling school, and that's been his dream and love. He worked very, very hard at it, and now he's one of the top wrestlers in the world."

And he's making more money than hockey players of his dad's era ever dreamed of:

"He says to me every day, 'I calculated out what you'd make now—that one year you got 26 goals, you'd be worth about $4 million today.' But, you know, I never regret anything. Emile Francis paid us very well. In those days, with inflation, we were paid very well, we were treated very well, and you couldn't give me the money in trade for the memories we had or the closeness of that hockey team. For six years, I'd died and gone to heaven, to play in the Big Apple with that group of guys—you can have all the money in the world, that's one of my greatest memories . . . the Billy Fairbairns and the Stemkowskis, and Eddie Giacomin and Whitey Villemure. All the guys. Brad Park always says to me, 'Why don't you write a book, Teddy?' because I can tell stories about all those guys and the fun we had on and off the ice."

On negotiating with Emile Francis:

"My first negotiation, I was on the second year of a contract. I came from Los Angeles, they weren't paying me a lot, and Emile renegotiated right away. He paid me $19,000 for two years. I had a pretty good year that one year, and I went in there in training camp, and I said, 'Emile, I'm making nineteen this year, but I think I deserve more, I had a pretty good year.' He says, 'Yeah, Teddy, you did, but you're under contract,' and he says, 'What are you gonna do if I don't sign you?' I said, 'I have a standing offer to go back home and work for another company.' He says, 'They're a great company and good luck to you,' and I went, 'Uh-oh.' He says, 'What do you think you're worth?' I said, 'I think I'm worth $25,000.' He says, 'Teddy, I'll give you $27,500.' I walked out of there, and I said to Billy Fairbairn, 'I think something's wrong, I think I was supposed to ask for $30,000, and they gave me $27,500. I don't think I'm supposed to ask for twenty-five and they give me twenty-seven-five.' He was more than fair with me.

"The following year he did the same thing for me and said, 'We want to keep you here,' and ripped up my contract. I got real bold and said I wanted points bonuses and stuff like that. He said, 'Teddy, I'll tell ya what, I'll give you an extra thousand dollars, forget the point bonuses.' He was a good, fair man to all of us."

On his greatest moment with the Rangers:

"I think the game we beat Boston in Boston, the fifth game [in 1972] when they had the Stanley Cup in the dressing room, and we came back. I was so proud of the guys when we left that building. I was proud of them there. I was proud of them some of the nights in Philadelphia, when we went out of that building and the fans were rocking our bus—I was proud of that. Those are memories I have—the year I got 26 goals, but more team stuff.

"I think the biggest thing is, I can remember games where we played in Vancouver, Los Angeles, and Oakland, any place we went everybody wanted a shot at the Big Apple, and the guys had to perform to another level. I remember we lost to Los Angeles, and we flew all the way to Montreal, and Montreal had a heck of a hockey club, and we had a brutal practice and we went into Montreal. I always thought, 'How the heck did we do that—right in the Montreal Forum, we beat them.' There were so many things I remember, but I think [playing for] the Stanley Cup was probably the highest moment of my career and the lowest at the same time. To this day, I can relive that game over and over again, with Bobby Orr taking that puck and the spin-a-rama. But the game before, when Bobby Rousseau scored, and we beat them in the Boston Garden, and they had the Stanley Cup in the dressing room and their napkins made up and everything else. I was really proud of the guys.

"That's the biggest thing I found about the Rangers—the guys stuck together and came up with some huge wins—and how guys fought back. Rod Gilbert wasn't the toughest guy in the world, Rod Seiling wasn't the toughest guy in the world, and they went into some buildings and guys ran the heck out of them. I know guys came looking for them."

On the things the players did to Emile Francis:

"We played in Los Angeles, and we were brutal. We flew all the way from Los Angeles to Montreal, and I'm afraid the guys had a little too much to drink on the airplane. We got to Montreal, we had a night off and a day off, but we hadn't played well, and Emile also knew we had a few drinks on the

Ted Irvine's famous son, wrestler Chris Jericho, loves to play hockey, too. Here, father and son get into it during a 2002 charity game. (Ronald Asadorian, Splashnews)

airplane. We're in Montreal, we went out for a nice dinner and a few more beers, and the next day at practice it was embarrassing. Emile stopped the practice, it was so embarrassing. We went and beat Montreal that night, and we were just quiet on the bus. Emile came on the bus, and he just said, 'Don't you guys ever do that to me again, play that bad and be so stupid off the ice.' As he sat down, his hat was crushed again. The guys used to crush his hat all the time, but that was a tough time to do it. Emile turns around and says, 'Chiefy or Rolfy, whoever did this,' and we all looked at these guys and said, 'Guys, don't get us in more trouble.'

"Then there was the time in Montreal, the reporters were looking for Emile Francis in the lobby of the hotel, and Stemmer said, 'Emile Francis is the only guy that goes up to his room with next year's draft list, compared to the rest of us—we go out looking for women.' But he got his hat crushed so many times. He knew it was going to be squashed, but he didn't say anything about it."

On the Rangers finally winning the Stanley Cup:

"For years, on the golf course, when I putted, I used to say to my partners, 'Don't put any pressure on me, we haven't won anything since '40.' Then, when these guys won it, I was very proud of them of. You're happy for the franchise. It's nice for the players, and Messier was so important, but the Ranger fans and the franchise, it takes the pressure off, because it's been a glorious franchise. Yes, you're proud. I went down in '98 and got an alumni ring, and I wear it to this day. My son Chris said, 'Dad, you don't wear jewelry.' I said, 'This one I will.'

"I remember the year we lost, 1971–72, the following year they had the Team Canada thing, and Team Canada came through here with Brad and Rod Seiling and Rod Gilbert and Vic Hadfield and Ratelle. I remember Don Awrey came over to our table when they played in Winnipeg and he stuck out his hand with this Stanley Cup ring, kind of 'just what you guys lost,' and we were all ready to deck him, but it was a Team Canada type of thing. And we lost, that was the difference—they had it and we didn't."

GILLES VILLEMURE'S CAREER RECORD

REGULAR SEASON

Year	Team / League	GP	Min	W	L	T	GA	GAA
58–59	Trios-Rivieres Reds QJHL							
	Troy Bruins IHL	3	180	1	2	0	18	6.00
59–60	Guelph Biltmores OHAJr	35	1980				128	3.66
60–61	New York Rovers EHL	51	3060	16	34	1	223	4.37
61–62	Long Island Ducks EHL	65	3900	25	39	1	242	3.72
	Charlotte Checkers EHL	1	60	0	1	0	7	7.00
	Johnstown Jets EHL	1	60	1	0	0	2	2.00
62–63	Vancouver Canucks WHL	70	4200	35	31	4	228	3.26
63–64	Baltimore Clippers AHL	66	3960	31	33	2	192	2.91
	New York Rangers NHL	5	300	0	2	3	18	3.60
64–65	Vancouver Canucks WHL	60	3676	27	26	6	212	3.46
65–66	Vancouver Canucks WHL	69	4178	32	34	3	223	3.20
66–67	Baltimore Clippers AHL	70	4180	34	27	9	238	3.42
67–68	New York Rangers NHL	4	200	1	2	0	8	2.40
	Buffalo Bisons AHL	37	2160	18	13	6	89	2.47
68–69	New York Rangers NHL	4	240	2	1	1	9	2.25
	Buffalo Bisons AHL	62	3674	36	12	14	148	2.42
69–70	Buffalo Bisons AHL	65	3714				156	2.52
70–71	New York Rangers NHL	34	2039	22	8	4	78	2.30
71–72	New York Rangers NHL	37	2129	24	7	4	74	2.09
72–73	New York Rangers NHL	34	2040	20	12	2	78	2.29
73–74	New York Rangers NHL	21	1054	7	7	3	62	3.53
74–75	New York Rangers NHL	45	2470	22	14	6	130	3.16
75–76	Chicago BlackHawks NHL	15	797	2	7	5	57	4.29
76–77	Chicago BlackHawks NHL	6	312	0	4	1	28	5.38
TEN (10) NHL SEASONS		205	11,581	100	64	29	542	2.81

POSTSEASON

Year	Team	GP	Min	W	L	GA	GAA
59–60	Guelph Biltmores OHAJr	5	300			19	3.80
62–63	Vancouver Canucks WHL	7	429	3	4	27	3.78
64–65	Vancouver Canucks WHL	5	309	1	4	17	3.30
65–66	Vancouver Canucks WHL	7	420	3	4	27	3.86
66–67	Baltimore Clippers AHL	9	569	4	5	39	4.11
67–68	Buffalo Bisons AHL	5	247	1	3	15	3.64
68–69	New York Rangers NHL	1	60	0	1	4	4.00
	Buffalo Bisons AHL	6	360	2	4	19	3.17
69–70	Buffalo Bisons AHL	14	875	11	3	31	2.13
70–71	New York Rangers NHL	2	80	0	1	6	4.50
71–72	New York Rangers NHL	6	360	4	2	14	2.33
72–73	New York Rangers NHL	2	61	0	1	2	1.97
73–74	New York Rangers NHL	1	1	0	0	0	0.00
74–75	New York Rangers NHL	2	94	1	0	6	3.83
SIX (6) NHL POSTSEASONS		14	656	5	5	32	2.93

NEW YORK RANGERS PLAYOFF RESULTS DURING GILLES VILLEMURE'S TIME WITH THE TEAM

1971

Game	Date	Opponent	Score	Result
1	Apr. 7	Toronto	5–4	W
2	8	Toronto	1–4	L
3	10	@Toronto	1–3	L
4	11	@Toronto	4–2	W
5	13	Toronto	3–1	W
6	15	@Toronto	2–1	W (ot)

Rangers won quarterfinals, 4–2

1	Apr. 18	@Chicago	2–1	W (ot)
2	20	@Chicago	0–3	L
3	22	Chicago	4–1	W
4	25	Chicago	1–7	L
5	27	@Chicago	2–3	L (ot)
6	29	Chicago	3–2	W (3 ot)
7	May 2	@Chicago	2–4	L

Blackhawks won semifinals, 4–3

1972

1	Apr. 5	Montreal	3–2	W
2	6	Montreal	5–2	W
3	8	@Montreal	1–2	L
4	9	@Montreal	6–4	W
5	11	Montreal	1–2	L
6	13	@Montreal	3–2	W

Rangers won quarterfinals, 4–2

1	Apr. 16	@Chicago	3–2	W
2	18	@Chicago	5–3	W
3	20	Chicago	3–2	W
4	23	Chicago	6–2	W

Rangers won semifinals, 4–0

Cont.

Game	Date	Opponent	Score	Result
1	Apr. 30	@Boston	5–6	L
2	May 2	@Boston	1–2	L
3	4	Boston	5–2	W
4	7	Boston	2–3	L
5	9	@Boston	3–2	W
6	11	Boston	0–3	L

Boston won finals, 4–2

1973

1	Apr. 4	@Boston	6–2	W
2	5	@Boston	4–2	W
3	7	Boston	2–4	L
4	8	Boston	4–0	W
5	10	@Boston	6–3	W

Rangers won quarterfinals, 4–1

1	Apr. 12	@Chicago	4–1	W
2	15	@Chicago	4–5	L
3	17	Chicago	1–2	L
4	19	Chicago	1–3	L
5	24	@Chicago	1–4	L

Blackhawks won semifinals, 4–1

1974

1	Apr. 10	@Montreal	4–1	W
2	11	@Montreal	1–4	L
3	13	Montreal	2–4	L
4	14	Montreal	6–4	W
5	16	@Montreal	3–2	W (ot)
6	18	Montreal	5–2	W

Rangers won quarterfinals, 4–2

Cont.

Game	Date	Opponent	Score	Result
1	Apr. 20	@Philadelphia	0–4	L
2	23	@Philadelphia	2–5	L
3	25	Philadelphia	5–3	W
4	28	Philadelphia	2–1	W (ot)
5	30	@Philadelphia	1–4	L
6	May 2	Philadelphia	4–1	W
7	5	@Philadelphia	3–4	L

Flyers won semifinals, 4–3

1975

1	Apr. 8	Islanders	2–3	L
2	10	@Islanders	8–3	W
3	11	Islanders	3–4	L (ot)

Islanders won preliminary round, 2–1

ALL-TIME RANGERS SHUTOUTS, INCLUDING PLAYOFFS (ENTERING THE 2015–16 SEASON)

Henrik Lundqvist	64
Ed Giacomin	50
Davey Kerr	47
John Ross Roach	35
Mike Richter	33
Chuck Rayner	25
Gump Worsley	24
Lorne Chabot	23
John Vanbiesbrouck	18
GILLES VILLEMURE	13

 Trivia Answers

#1 *Jaromir Jagr holds the Rangers record for power-play goals in a season, with 24 in 2005–06, breaking Vic Hadfield's record of 23, set in 1971–72.*

#2 *Gump Worsley is third on the all-time list (Eddie Giacomin is No. 4 and I am No. 9).*

#3 *The Chicago Blackhawks are the only one of the original six the Rangers haven't faced in the finals. The Blueshirts have met Toronto three times, Detroit and Boston twice each, and Montreal once. Toronto is the only one of the group the Rangers have beaten in a final series, and it happened twice (1933 and 1940).*

#4 John Vanbiesbrouck in 1985–85 and Henrik Lundqvist in 2011–12.

#5 Walter Tkaczuk has played in more playoff games than any other Ranger, 93.

#6 Sergei Zubov's 89 points in 1993–94 (the Stanley Cup season) ranks second on the Rangers' all-time list for points in a season by a defenseman, while Brad Park's 82 in 1973–74 was fifth.

#7 The Rangers beat the Los Angeles Kings, New York Islanders, and Philadelphia Flyers to reach the 1979 Stanley Cup finals, going 10–3 before winning the first game of the finals series against Montreal and then losing four straight to come up short again.

#8 After the three members of the 1,000-game club, defenseman/center Ron Greschner is next on the Rangers' all-time list, playing in 982 games.

#9 Pierre Jarry and Don Maloney are the two Rangers who scored goals eight seconds apart. Jarry scored at 11:03 and 11:11 of the third period against California on November 21, 1971 at Madison Square Garden, and Maloney tallied at 12:48 and 12:56 of the third at Philadelphia, March 12, 1987.

#10 *Mike Richter played 45 games during the 2000–01 season, while Kirk McLean appeared in 23, Guy Hebert in 13, Vitali Yeremyev in 4, Johan Holmqvist in 2, and Jason LaBarbara in 1.*